The
Eternal Companion

BOOKS BY SWAMI PRABHAVANANDA

Original Works

THE SERMON ON THE MOUNT ACCORDING TO
   VEDANTA
RELIGION IN PRACTICE
YOGA AND MYSTICISM
THE SPIRITUAL HERITAGE OF INDIA
   (*with Frederick Manchester*)
VEDIC RELIGION AND PHILOSOPHY

Translations

THE WISDOM OF GOD (*Srimad Bhagavatam*)
SHANKARA'S CREST-JEWEL OF DISCRIMINATION
   (*with Christopher Isherwood*)
THE UPANISHADS (*with Frederick Manchester*)
THE SONG OF GOD: BHAGAVAD-GITA
   (*with Isherwood*)
HOW TO KNOW GOD, THE YOGA APHORISMS OF
   PATANJALI (*with Isherwood*)
SWAMI PREMANANDA: TEACHINGS AND
   REMINISCENCES

THE ETERNAL
COMPANION

BRAHMANANDA

Teachings and Reminiscences
with a Biography by

SWAMI PRABHAVANANDA

VEDANTA PRESS
Hollywood, California

Paperback edition: ISBN 0-87481-024-8
Library of Congress Catalog Card Number: 72-113256

First Edition, 1944
Third Edition, Revised and enlarged, 1970
7 8 9 10 11 12 13 14 15

Printed in the United States of America
On acid-free paper
to meet the guidelines of the Council of Library Resources

If you wish to learn in greater detail about the
teachings within this book,
e-mail us at info@vedanta.org
        or
Contact the Secretary, Vedanta Society, 1946
Vedanta Pl., Hollywood CA 90068 USA
phone: 323-465-7114

You can also visit our web sites:
www.vedanta.com - for information on our books
and free excerpts of our books
info@vedanta.com - for questions or to ask for a
catalog
www.vedanta.org -for general information on
Vedanta philosophy and a list of our centers
info@vedanta.org - for questions about Vedanta
philosophy

CONTENTS

PREFACE

Sʀɪ Rᴀᴍᴀᴋʀɪsʜɴᴀ's name has already become a household word in India, and the inspiration of his life and teachings is beginning to be felt in the West. Two of Ramakrishna's greatest disciples were Swami Vivekananda and Swami Brahmananda. Swami Vivekananda carried the message of Vedanta to America and Europe. Brahmananda was regarded by Ramakrishna as his spiritual son. He became the first head of the monastic order of Ramakrishna.

In writing the biographical part of this book on Swami Brahmananda, I have used much of the material contained in the Bengali life published by the Udbodhan Office, Calcutta, India. To this I have added the personal reminiscences of Swamis Yatiswarananda, Akhilananda, Vishwananda, and other swamis and devotees—as well as my own.

The teachings contained in this volume have been

translated from the original Bengali edition, also published by the Udbodhan Office. They are taken from diaries, private notes, and memories of informal talks given to young monastic disciples on various occasions.

PRABHAVANANDA

Hollywood, March 1944

PREFACE TO 1970 EDITION

For this new edition, beyond my own revisions, I have incorporated reminiscences contributed by Swami Brahmananda's monastic and householder disciples and originally published in *Vedanta and the West*. Some previously unrecorded memories have also been included.

PRABHAVANANDA

Hollywood, January 1970

The
Eternal Companion

INTRODUCTION

To write the biography of an illumined soul is very difficult, if not impossible; for his is preeminently an inner life. True, he may engage in certain external activities; he may achieve the kind of success which impresses the outer world; but all these activities and achievements—including even his spoken and written teachings—will fall far short of, and fail to express, the real man.

An ordinary professor or scholar teaches out of his accumulated learning. Such a man's scholarship is far greater than the man himself. That is to say, he may teach the loftiest truths, theoretically, without having made them a part of his own life and experience. A man of spiritual wisdom also teaches these truths, not theoretically, but out of his own experience. Nevertheless, the expression of these truths in words cannot possibly correspond to the vastness of his inner knowledge, which is inexpressible because it is transcendental. We know a man with our mind and senses; but our mind and senses cannot reveal to us the nature of an illumined soul. In order to be able fully to understand such a soul a man must himself be illumined.

When you go into the presence of one of these great beings, something very wonderful happens. His mere presence gives you, as it were, a supersense which enables you to recognize the greatness which is in him. Maharaj (as Swami Brahmananda was called) used to give us that supersense whenever we were with him. Our minds were lifted up and caught glimpses of his inner nature; but these glimpses were only partial. We were aware that the other disciples of Sri Ramakrishna, who were themselves illumined souls, could see more in Maharaj than we, his disciples, ever saw. Swami Ramakrishnananda, founder and head of the Ramakrishna Monastery in Madras, once introduced Maharaj to his disciples there, saying: "None of you have seen Sri Ramakrishna himself; but now you see Maharaj, and that is the same thing." On another occasion a devotee brought fruit which he wanted to offer to Sri Ramakrishna in the shrine. Swami Ramakrishnananda told him to offer it to Maharaj, and said: "To offer this fruit to Maharaj is as good as offering it to Sri Ramakrishna."

One day I hesitated to accept something that Maharaj told me. Swami Shivananda was present at the time, and he agreed with Maharaj immediately. I did not like this. Later I talked to Swami Shivananda alone and more or less accused him of being a "yes-man" to Maharaj. Swami Shivananda laughed and said: "My boy, you see in Maharaj only Maharaj; but we see the external form of Maharaj with nothing inside it but God. Whatever Maharaj tells you comes directly from God."

It should be remembered that this statement was not made by a mere ignorant enthusiast, but by one who was himself an illumined soul. Its truth was not clear to me at the time, but later I began to understand and believe it because of a talk which I had with Maharaj himself. One day he asked me to look at the almanac and find an auspicious date for his departure from Madras. As I did so, I could not help smiling. Maharaj noticed this and asked me why I was amused. I replied: "Well, Maharaj, you always go through this routine whenever you plan to go anywhere, but then you suddenly make up your mind to leave on some other day."

At this Maharaj said: "Do you think I do anything according to my own will? The devotees insist upon fixing some date for my going, so to avoid constant pestering I fix a tentative date. But I do not move or do anything until I know the will of the Lord."

"Do you mean to say," I asked, "that you are al ways guided by the will of God?"

Maharaj: "Yes."

Myself: "Well, Maharaj, I too may think or feel that I am doing the will of God, when actually I am only following my own inclinations and attributing them to God's will. Isn't that what you do?"

Maharaj: "No, my child, it is not the same."

Myself: "Then do you mean to say that you actually see God and talk to him directly and know his will?"

Maharaj: "Yes, I wait until I know his will directly and he tells me what I should do."

Myself: "For everything you do?"

Maharaj: "Yes, for everything I do I have the direct guidance of God."

Myself: "And do you accept only those disciples he wants you to accept?"

Maharaj: "Yes."

After this talk with him I began to find some meaning in his peculiar way of acting. For example, whenever any of us would ask his advice, he would say: "Wait. My brain is not working today," or: "My stomach is upset, I'll answer tomorrow." Sometimes many tomorrows would pass before the disciple got any definite answer. But when Maharaj did finally speak there was always a special power behind his words.

"How does he know the will of God? Does he go into *samadhi* every time before he knows it?" This was the thought that continually crossed my mind. But, not daring to ask him, I waited, hoping somehow to get an answer. Then, one day, I was discussing with another disciple the spiritual visions of "Gopal's Mother," a woman disciple of Sri Ramakrishna. She had been given this name because she used to see Gopal, the boy Krishna, playing with her, walking beside her, and calling her "Mother." I expressed my opinion that these visions of "Gopal's Mother" belonged to the transcendental plane, and that I did not believe she had actually seen Sri Krishna with her physical eyes. Maharaj, who was sitting in his room, overheard me. He came out and said rather sarcastically: "Ah! So you are omniscient!"

"But Maharaj," I asked, "how can one see God in the external world with physical eyes?"

Maharaj simply made this statement in English: "Show me the line of demarcation where matter ends and spirit begins."

In other words, I understood him to say that when the eye of the spirit opens one sees *Brahman* everywhere.

The following teachings of Shankara in his *Viveka-Chudamani* (*Crest-Jewel of Discrimination*) elucidate the above remark of Maharaj:

"Our perception of the universe is a continuous perception of Brahman, though the ignorant man is not aware of this. Indeed, this universe is nothing but Brahman. See Brahman everywhere, under all circumstances, with the eye of the spirit and a tranquil heart. How can the physical eyes see anything but physical objects? How can the mind of the enlightened man think of anything other than the Reality?"

In the Upanishads we read that "a knower of Brahman becomes Brahman." What is it that attracts people to a man of God? Young and old, boys and girls, men, women and children, saints and sinners—all felt an indefinable attraction to Maharaj, even if they did not in the least understand what was meant by "a knower of Brahman."

When I first met Maharaj I was a boy of eighteen. I did not know anything about God or the realization of God, yet I felt drawn to him as to a long-lost friend who was very near and dear to me. I had never felt such a love before in my life: it was the love of parents and the love of a friend, all in one. Everyone had the same experience. Once I asked Swami Subodhananda, another disciple of Sri Ramakrishna, the reason for this all-satisfying love which emanated from Maharaj. The Swami replied: "God is love. Maharaj has realized God. Therefore he is full of love."

You did not have to be pure-hearted or spiritually minded to love Maharaj. Even the most depraved natures felt this love when they came into his presence, and many of them were transformed into saints. Maharaj did not talk to everybody about God or spiritual matters or philosophical truths; he would come down, as it were, to the level of each individual; he became that person. He had the power to uplift a man without his even knowing it; and when that person left his presence he was bathed in love and purity. When you were in the presence of Maharaj you completely forgot yourself. You felt you were in another world where there was no worry or grief, and where man was not man but divine. You were filled with a peculiar joy which you could neither explain nor understand.

Maharaj's bearing was stately and regal. He was tall and well-built, and his face was serene and joyful. His eyes were deep, and seemed always to be gazing into the infinite. Whenever he looked at you, you felt that he was probing the depths of your innermost nature and that he knew all your weaknesses and failings. But somehow you did not mind this being known through and through because those eyes were so full of mercy and love. We never feared to be known by him. Then there were other times when, though his eyes were wide open, it seemed as if the universe no longer existed for him; he seemed to be living in a different world altogether.

His hands and feet were beautifully formed, and they possessed a peculiar attraction. His back strikingly resembled the back of Sri Ramakrishna. Swami Turiyananda once told me how, many years after the passing away of Sri Ramakrishna, he saw Maharaj from behind, walking in the grounds of the Belur Monastery, and mistook him for Sri Ramakrishna himself.

Once in a crowded railway station I overheard a man who had been observing Maharaj exclaim to a friend: "Look at that man! What part of India does he come from? He isn't like a Madrasi, or a Parsi, or a Bengali, or a Punjabi. Can you guess his nationality?"

And the other answered: "No, I can't. But you can see very well that he is a man of God."

The Life of Maharaj

I

CHILDHOOD AND EARLY YEARS

SWAMI BRAHMANANDA was born on January 21, 1863, at Sikra, a village near Calcutta, Bengal. His parents were Ananda Mohan Ghosh and Kailas Kamini. Kailas Kamini, his mother, was devoted to Krishna and she spent most of her time in prayer, worship, and meditation. Maharaj was her only son. Being a devotee of Krishna, she named him Rakhal, "the shepherd boy." She passed away when Rakhal was five years old.

Rakhal liked being with other children and played all kinds of games with them. He was especially fond of "playing church." He would mold a clay image of the Divine Mother and worship her with his playmates. During religious festivals he would take his seat behind the priest, and sometimes while watching the worship he would be filled with a fervor of devotion and become absorbed in the thought of the Divine Mother.

Ananda Mohan loved gardening. As a child,

Rakhal would work with his father, and learned gardening from him at an early age. He was also fond of fishing and would sit patiently with his fishing rod for hours by the pond. Even in later life, we saw that he had never lost these two early enthusiasms of childhood—gardening and fishing.

From boyhood, he was a lover of music. He learned songs about the Divine Mother and Krishna. He and his friends would go into a mango grove and sing these songs together in chorus. In later years he encouraged his disciples to sing devotional songs, and he would always keep in his company a few who were expert musicians. Wherever he went, praises of the Lord would be sung.

When Rakhal had finished his studies at the village primary school, he went to Calcutta to begin grammar school. He was then twelve years old. Attached to this school was an athletic club, which interested Rakhal very much. The members of the club were young boys, and Naren (later known as Vivekananda) was their leader. This was how Rakhal and Naren met. They were of the same age and became very fond of each other. Later both boys became pupils at a gymnasium directed by a Mr. Guha.

At this period Keshab Chandra Sen was exercising a great influence over the youth of Bengal by his powerful oratory, his fervent devotion, and his vast knowledge of Eastern and Western religions. He was the leader of the Brahmo Samaj. He preached the fatherhood of God and the brotherhood of man. In his talks, he would quote the Upanishads and the Christian Bible; his new line of approach revived an interest in religion among the educated classes of Bengal. The creed of the Brahmo Samaj was the theistic conception of the Godhead which is the only creed of Christianity and which is also to be found, among many other conceptions, in the Hindu scriptures. Keshab denounced as polytheism the Hindu cult of many gods and goddesses, although these are, in reality, merely aspects of the one Brahman. He was opposed to the worship of images in the temples. Naren and Rakhal joined the movement and subscribed to its creed.

Rakhal used to spend most of his time in prayer and contemplation, neglecting his studies. "God is our Father, our very own. How shall I reach him?" This was the only thought that occupied his mind. Sri Ramakrishna later used to say of him: "Rakhal was born with an intense love for God. Such a love is usually acquired only after a man has practiced spiritual disciplines for many years or many lives." Rakhal regularly attended the services of the Brahmo Samaj. His prayer that God might be revealed to him continued incessantly, like the act of breathing.

Rakhal was not doing very well at school, so that, by the time he reached his sixteenth birthday, his father was worried about the boy's future. He attributed the neglect of his studies to the emotionalism of adolescence which had turned his son's mind toward God. If Rakhal were married, the father thought to himself, his mind would be brought down to earth. He would have to consider taking up a career and providing for his wife, and therefore he would study harder. So he arranged for Rakhal's marriage to a young girl named Visweswari.

Keshab Chandra Sen was the first to preach publicly the greatness of Sri Ramakrishna. Devotees began to flock to the temple at Dakshineswar to visit the Master. Among them were Manomohan Mitra and Shyama Sundari, the brother and mother of Visweswari. At the time of Rakhal's marriage, these two were already ardent devotees of Sri Ramakrishna, whom they regarded as an incarnation of Sri Chaitanya. Thus it came about that the worldly influence of marriage combined with the spiritual influence of Keshab brought Rakhal to the feet of his future beloved master.

It was natural that Manomohan should introduce Rakhal, his new brother-in-law, to Sri Ramakrishna. For some time before their visit, the Master had spiritual visions concerning his future disciple. Once Sri Ramakrishna prayed to the Divine Mother: "Mother, I want someone to be my constant companion. Bring me a boy who is pure-hearted and intensely devoted to you." A few days later he saw in mystic vision a boy standing under the banyan tree in the temple grounds. On another occasion, this same boy appeared to him in a different manner. To quote the Master's own words: "A few days before Rakhal came to me Mother placed a little boy on my lap and said: 'This is your son.' At first I was startled. 'My son?' Mother smiled at this and made me understand that I was not to have a son in the ordinary sense but that this boy would be my spiritual son, one who would live up to the highest ideal of renunciation."

From this hour onward, Sri Ramakrishna waited eagerly for the coming of his spiritual son. A few moments before Rakhal actually arrived he had another vision. Suddenly he saw a hundred-petaled lotus blooming on the bosom of the Ganges, each of its petals shining with exquisite loveliness. On the lotus two boys were dancing with anklets on their feet. One of them was Sri Krishna himself; the other was the same boy he had seen in his earlier vision. Their dance was indescribably beautiful; every movement they made seemed to splash foam, as it were, from an ocean of sweetness. Sri Ramakrishna was lost in ecstasy.

Just then a boat arrived carrying Manomohan and Rakhal. Sri Ramakrishna looked at Rakhal in bewilderment. "What is this?" he thought to himself: "Here is the boy I saw standing under the banyan tree; here is the boy Mother placed on my lap; here is the boy I saw just now dancing on the lotus with Sri Krishna. This is the pure-hearted companion I prayed for to Mother."

Sri Ramakrishna regarded Rakhal for a few moments in silence. Then he smilingly remarked to Manomohan: "There are wonderful possibilities in this boy." After this, the Master talked to Rakhal for some time, as though he were an old friend.

"What is your name?" he asked.

Rakhal answered: "Rakhal Chandra Ghosh."

Hearing the name "Rakhal," Sri Ramakrishna was deeply excited, and muttered to himself: "Rakhal! The shepherd boy of Brindaban—the playmate of Sri Krishna!"

Then, in a sweet affectionate voice, he said: "Come and see me again."

In the presence of the Master, Rakhal had experienced a peculiar feeling of joy, love, and intense attraction. As he left the temple grounds, that voice in all its sweetness kept echoing within his heart: "Come and see me again." He knew that at last he had met a man who had seen and known God.

Rakhal went back to his home and to school, but he could not forget his visit to the Master. Sri Ramakrishna filled all his thoughts, and he was impatient to see him again. A few days later, after school hours, he went alone to Dakshineswar. The Master welcomed him eagerly and said with great affection: "Why didn't you come back to me sooner? I have been waiting for you." Rakhal did not know what to answer. He looked at the Master and felt that same ecstatic joy. He felt like a little child sitting at the feet of God, the Father of all. From that day onward, the relationship between these two was established. Rakhal saw in Ramakrishna father, mother, and God. Sri Ramakrishna saw in Rakhal the Divine Child.

Rakhal's visits to the Master became more and more frequent. Sometimes he lived at the temple for days together. While he was there, his mind entirely forgot the everyday world and became absorbed in the consciousness of God and his presence. He felt himself to be the eternal companion of his divine master.

Recalling these early days with Rakhal, Sri Ramakrishna used to tell his intimate disciples: "No words can describe Rakhal's spiritual mood during that period. He was living in a state of ecstasy most of the time. He was like a little child, helpless in its mother's arms and surrendering itself completely to her—always conscious of the divine relationship. And when he was near me, I also was transported into a higher spiritual consciousness. I used to play with him, just as Yasoda, the Divine Mother, played with her Divine Child, Krishna."

Rakhal's father tried in many ways to bring his son's mind back to the interests of worldly life. He gave him strict orders not to go to the temple at Dakshineswar. When his advice and threats proved of no avail, he had Rakhal locked in the house. Rakhal longed to go to his master, and Sri Ramakrishna prayed earnestly to the Divine Mother that all the obstacles in Rakhal's spiritual path might be removed.

One day, Ananda Mohan made Rakhal sit beside him in his study while he looked over some legal documents. As soon as Rakhal noticed that his father was deeply absorbed in the work, he seized the opportunity to slip out of the room and hurried off to his master.

Ananda Mohan knew that Rakhal must have gone to Sri Ramakrishna, but for some days he could do nothing, because he had to attend to a lawsuit in the courts. As soon as he had time, however, he went to Dakshineswar, intending to take his son home. When Rakhal saw his father coming, he was frightened and wanted to hide, but Sri Ramakrishna would not let him. So Rakhal, following his master's advice, went to meet his father and greeted him with unusual affection and reverence. It was then that Ananda Mohan had a change of heart. Instead of insisting on Rakhal's returning home, he simply requested Sri Ramakrishna to send the boy occasionally to see him.

II

LIFE WITH RAMAKRISHNA

RAKHAL BEGAN LIVING with the Master at Dak-shineswar. One day his young wife came to the temple with her mother. Looking at her Sri Ramakrishna said: "She is born with a divine nature. She will never be an obstacle to Rakhal's spiritual progress." The Master then sent word to Holy Mother, who was also living at the temple, that she should bless the young girl and welcome her as her daughter-in-law. After receiving the blessings, the mother and daughter returned home.

Rakhal, with a carefree mind, devoted himself to a contemplative life and the service of his beloved *guru.*

One day, Rakhal told Sri Ramakrishna that he felt very hungry but there was no food in the place. Sri Ramakrishna became greatly concerned. Leaving his room, he went to the bank of the Ganges and shouted: "O Gourdasi, come soon! My Rakhal is hungry!" Shortly after this, Gourdasi, a woman disciple of Sri Ramakrishna, arrived by boat with a few other disciples, bringing food. Sri Ramakrishna was as happy as a child and called Rakhal, saying: "Here's food, now go and eat. You are very hungry."

Rakhal felt embarrassed and said in a low voice: "Yes, I *am* hungry—but do you have to advertise it?"

Sri Ramakrishna innocently replied: "If you are hungry, what is wrong in saying so? Go and eat now."

Once, while Rakhal was massaging Sri Ramakrishna with oil, he begged the Master to grant him the power of transcendental vision. At first Sri Ramakrishna took no notice of his request and remained silent. When Rakhal persisted, the Master suddenly turned and spoke to him very harshly. Rakhal felt hurt and angry. He smashed the bottle of oil on the ground and ran away, but, as he reached the gate of the temple, his feet suddenly seemed paralyzed. He could not move another step. Helplessly he sat down on the road, not knowing what to do. Meanwhile, Sri Ramakrishna sent his nephew, Ramlal, to find Rakhal and calm his anger. Ramlal fetched Rakhal, who slowly returned to the Master's presence. Sri Ramakrishna looked at him smilingly: "You see! You could not go outside that circle I drew around you!" Rakhal felt ashamed and remained silent. A few moments later, Sri Ramakrishna went into ecstasy and began to speak to the Divine Mother. "O Mother," he murmured, "I know you have given him one-sixteenth part of your power; and that power in him will benefit all mankind."

Then, in the same ecstatic mood, he addressed Rakhal, saying: "You were angry with me. Do you know why I made you angry? There was a purpose in it. Medicine acts only after the sore has been opened." He continued: "Have faith that God is also with form and can be seen in that way. God is revealed to the man who has controlled his mind."

A few days later, while massaging his master's feet, Rakhal suddenly lost his external senses and was transported into that transcendental realm which he had longed to experience. In later years, Sri Ramakrishna used to point out the exact spot in the room where Rakhal went into samadhi for the first time.

Naren (Vivekananda) met Sri Ramakrishna about six months after Rakhal's arrival. Rakhal and Naren were happy to be together again at the feet of their master. But one day Naren was shocked when he saw Rakhal follow Sri Ramakrishna into the temple of Mother Kali and prostrate before the image. He remembered how Rakhal had signed the pledge of the Brahmo Samaj, promising not to worship images or forms of God. At the first opportunity, Naren reminded Rakhal of his promise and reproached him bitterly for indulging in image-worship. Rakhal was silent. How could he ever make Naren understand what he had experienced through his master's grace? Yet he could not argue the matter. So, for a few days, Rakhal avoided Naren, and Naren would not speak to Rakhal. Sri Ramakrishna noticed this, and when he learned the reason for the quarrel he talked affectionately to Naren and made him realize that Rakhal was not responsible for the change in his attitude toward images. After that the boys became friends again.

Two years passed away in the holy company of Sri Ramakrishna, during which time Rakhal lived such an intensely spiritual inner life that he forgot all about his duty to his young wife. Shyama Sundari, his mother-in-law, understood him, however, because of her own devotion to Sri Ramakrishna. Knowing how pure and how devoted to God Rakhal was, she trained her daughter to be a worthy wife. A neighbor once said to her: "It seems your son-in-law is turning into a monk. Why don't you try to bring his mind back to the world, for your daughter's sake?"

"What can I do?" Shyama Sundari answered. "Everything depends on the will of the Lord. If my son-in-law becomes a monk, I shall regard it as a great blessing."

Soon after this, Shyama Sundari came with her daughter to visit Rakhal and asked him to return home. The meeting took place in the presence of Sri Ramakrishna, who remained silent throughout Later, the Master described it to his other disciples and said: "Rakhal has now reached true spiritual discrimination. I know he will no longer be attached to the world. He has realized the emptiness of earthly pleasures."

The Master felt, however, that Rakhal had a duty to his wife, and told him to visit her from time to time. Rakhal obeyed. Gradually, his visits to his wife became longer; he felt concerned about her and her future. Finally he came to Sri Ramakrishna and asked his advice. The Master listened to everything he had to say but refused to tell him definitely which path of life he should follow. With a heavy heart Rakhal went back to his wife and silently prayed to Sri Ramakrishna to show him the way. Three days passed. Rakhal prayed unceasingly. Suddenly, a veil was removed from his sight and he saw the divine *maya* —the play of the Divine Mother. He knew now which path to choose. He and his wife were not to be bound by the ties of marriage. He had a great mission to fulfill. He was certain, now, that his wife would be taken care of; and, strangely enough, she also felt full of peace. So, taking leave of her, he went straight back to Dakshineswar. The Master knew exactly what had happened. Silently smiling, he welcomed home his beloved spiritual son.

Sri Ramakrishna had known that Rakhal could not be bound by any earthly attachment. Yet there remained in him a subtle, lingering desire, a desire which could not be completely removed from his heart until it had had some satisfaction. That was why Sri Ramakrishna had sent Rakhal back to his wife. Now he knew that, henceforward, Rakhal would be completely free from desire in any form.

Sri Ramakrishna used to say: "The virtue of truthfulness is most important. If a man always speaks the truth and holds to the truth tenaciously, he will realize God; for God is Truth. I prayed to the Divine Mother, saying: 'Mother, here is knowledge, here is ignorance—take them both and give me pure love for you. Here is purity, here is impurity—take them both and give me pure love for you. Here is good, here is evil—take them both and give me pure love for you.' But I could not say, 'Here is truth, here is untruth— take them both.' "

One day, Sri Ramakrishna said to Rakhal: "I can't look at you. I see a veil of ignorance over your face. Tell me, have you done anything wrong?"

Rakhal was greatly troubled. No matter how hard he tried, he could not remember having done anything wrong. "Try to recall," Sri Ramakrishna said to his disciple, "if you have told any untruth." Rakhal at once remembered and admitted that he had recently told a lie in a joking way to a friend. Sri Ramakrishna forgave him, but said: "Never do it again. To speak the exact truth always is a most important spiritual discipline."

Rakhal's enthusiasm for the spiritual life did not weaken, but after a while he ceased to meditate regularly. Sri Ramakrishna noticed this and asked him the reason. Rakhal answered: "I do not always get the inspiration. My heart seems dry, and I feel an emptiness."

"You must never neglect your meditation on that account," Sri Ramakrishna told him. "Make up your mind to practice spiritual disciplines, then the enthusiasm will come naturally. Those who are farmers by birth and occupation do not and cannot give up farming just because the crops fail. So you must not give up meditation even though you may not get any apparent results. You must be regular in your practice."

That same day, Sri Ramakrishna went as usual to worship in the temple. Rakhal followed him, and sat down to meditate in the hall facing the shrine. Suddenly he saw the shrine grow strangely luminous. The illumination increased in strength until it was as bright as the sun itself, but mellow, not dazzling. This light began to pour through the door of the shrine and seemed about to engulf Rakhal. He was on the verge of losing consciousness. The sensation frightened him. He got up and went out.

Later, Sri Ramakrishna found him sitting silently in his room. "Why did you run away?" the Master asked. "You complain that your heart is dry and you don't have any more spiritual visions, yet you are afraid to experience anything. That's not right."

A few days after this, Rakhal was sitting absorbed in meditation in the hall of the temple and experiencing an ecstatic joy. Sri Ramakrishna approached him in ecstasy and gave him a special *mantram* for his own use. "Look," said the Master, "there is your Chosen Ideal!" Rakhal in ecstatic vision saw his chosen aspect of the Godhead standing before him— living and luminous, with a smile playing on his lips. When Rakhal regained his external consciousness and saw Sri Ramakrishna, he prostrated at his feet with loving devotion. He had known and experienced the divine power and grace of his guru. Sri Rama-krishna returned to his room, and Rakhal became once more absorbed in meditation.

On another occasion, while Rakhal was meditat-ing, his mind became very dry and restless. All his struggles to calm it were of no avail. Disheartened, and disappointed at his own failure, he rose from his seat. Then Sri Ramakrishna came to him and said: "I see an obstacle on your path. Put out your tongue." Rakhal obeyed. The Master drew some lines on his disciple's tongue with his finger and said: "Now go and meditate." At once Rakhal found himself freed from his distractions.

During this period, Sri Ramakrishna taught his dis-ciple many kinds of spiritual disciplines, and Rakhal used to practice them with great earnestness—but always in privacy and solitude. Often, when Sri Ramakrishna and his devotees were together, a mood of spiritual fervor would come over the whole group. Then Rakhal would go into ecstasy. Once, at the house of Balaram, a disciple of Sri Ramakrishna, the devotees were chanting the name of God, and the Master was in samadhi. Rakhal was in ecstasy, appar-ently unconscious. When Sri Ramakrishna came out of samadhi, he touched Rakhal on the heart and thus brought him back to normal consciousness.

In *The Gospel of Sri Ramakrishna*, "M." (a close disciple) records some remarks the Master made about Rakhal's spiritual condition at this time:

"Rakhal has grown into a very sweet character

now. He practices *japam* unceasingly—that is the reason you see his lips moving sometimes. When I look at him and notice his mental condition, I often feel inspired and lose myself in ecstasy.

"Naren, Rakhal, and a few others belong to the class of the 'Ever-perfect.' They are born with God-knowledge. As they begin to grow up, they realize the emptiness of earthly pleasures. The Vedas tell us of a bird called the homa. This bird lives high in the sky: it never comes down to earth. It lays its eggs in mid-air, but at such a great height that the eggs hatch while still falling. The little bird comes out and finds itself dashing down toward the earth. When it sees the ground rushing to meet it, it soars up and rejoins its mother in the sky.

"Boys like Rakhal resemble the homa. From their earliest childhood they see the emptiness of the world and their one thought is how to reach God."

Sri Ramakrishna also remarked: "Rakhal at one time became very sensitive to people. He could not bear the sight of those who were worldly-minded. I, too, went through the same mood at one time. Rakhal had another mood in which he loved to be alone and taste the divine bliss in complete absorption. At such times, he told me, he could not bear even my company. He came here to look after me, but while he was passing through this stage I had to look after him."

During this period, Rakhal had many visions and developed various occult powers. But, following his

master's advice, he learned to pay no attention to
them.

To quote his own words: "While I was with the
Master, a man who was living in the temple fell sick.
He had no one to look after him, so I nursed him for
a few days. One night, when I was sitting beside him,
his suffering became intense. I did not know how to
help him, so I thought I would repeat the Lord's name
and pray for his relief. After I had practiced japam for
some time, a kind of slumber overcame me. In that
state I saw a beautiful young girl, about twelve years
old, standing before me. She had the look of a goddess. I asked her: 'Mother, will this man be cured?'
She nodded and answered: 'Yes.' The vision disappeared instantly. Next day, the patient recovered."

Just as the inside of a cupboard can be seen through
its glass doors, so Rakhal could see into any man's
heart. He was aware of the character and motives of
everybody who visited the temple, and would refuse
to allow any but sincere, earnest people to enter the
Master's presence. Sri Ramakrishna learned that
Rakhal possessed this power, and that he was using
it. He scolded him severely, saying: "It is mean to use
your power this way. He who pays heed to occult
powers cannot live in God-knowledge. Take no notice of such powers when they come to you."

In later years, a man once complained to Swami
Sharvananda, a disciple of Maharaj, that they were
not really holy men because they did not possess
occult powers. When this was reported to Maharaj,

he said: "It is easy to acquire occult powers, but hard indeed to attain purity of heart. To find purity of heart is to know the real truth of religion."

There now arose a new obstacle to Rakhal's continuous stay with the Master. He became sick, and was sent to Calcutta to live in the house of Balaram. Sri Ramakrishna wanted Balaram to take particular care of his disciple and told him: "Boys like Naren and Rakhal are born for a divine mission. To serve them is to serve God." Balaram felt very happy to serve his master's spiritual child. But the climate of Calcutta did not agree with Rakhal, so, with the permission of Sri Ramakrishna, Balaram took him to Brindaban for a change of air. At first, Rakhal felt better. He found Brindaban very inspiring and wrote highly of it to "M": "What a wonderful holy place is Brindaban! The wild peacocks are dancing all around. The air is full of singing and dancing and the praises of the Lord. Here you feel an unending joy in the holy Name!" Then he became seriously ill. This troubled the Master. To quote Sri Ramakrishna's own words: "I was extremely worried when I learned of Rakhal's illness at Brindaban. Brindaban is the holy place where Sri Krishna spent his youth. Since Mother revealed to me that Rakhal is the playmate of Sri Krishna and one of the shepherd boys of Brindaban, I was afraid lest he should be reminded of his past incarnation. If he remembered his association with Sri Krishna while at Brindaban, he might give up his body there. Therefore I prayed fervently to the

Divine Mother, and she assured me that I had no cause for anxiety."

The Gospel of Sri Ramakrishna contains this reference to Rakhal's illness:

"Sri Ramakrishna speaks of Rakhal: 'While massaging my feet, Rakhal had his first ecstasy here. A scholar was with me, expounding the Bhagavatam. As Rakhal listened to the words of the scripture, he began to feel ecstatic joy. Then he lost consciousness and became absorbed in samadhi.

" 'He attained samadhi for the second time at Balaram's house. He fell on the ground, apparently unconscious. Rakhal is a devotee of a very high order —he dwells in the realm of the personal aspect of God. If he hears people talking about the impersonal, he goes out of the room.

" 'I prayed to the Divine Mother for his recovery. He has renounced everything and he depends entirely on me.

" 'When he first went to Brindaban, he wrote to M., saying how wonderful the place is and how the peacocks are dancing around; but now those peacocks seem to hold no charm for him.

" 'Why do I love these boys so much? Because their hearts are so pure.' "

When Rakhal returned from Brindaban, he found that many new disciples had gathered around the Master; among them he saw many of his old school friends. Soon after this, Sri Ramakrishna fell ill and was finally removed to the Cossipore garden house.

Rakhal accompanied him. One after another, several of the young disciples went to live there and look after the Master. It was during this last illness that Sri Ramakrishna established his monastic order, and fired his young disciples with the ideal of renunciation. He began to train each one individually, according to his character and temperament. To some he gave the *gerua* cloth, which symbolizes the life of renunciation. Naren and Rakhal were among these chosen few.

The Master was undoubtedly a very sick man, but he still remained the source and center of a strong spiritual current which transformed the lives and characters of those around him. The Cossipore garden house became a place of bliss, and the disciples' hearts overflowed with joy in God.

It was during this period that Sri Ramakrishna prepared Naren to deliver his message to mankind. He taught him how to train the young disciples and organize the monastic order. Every day he would talk to Naren for hours together. In the course of one conversation he told him: "Rakhal has the keen intelligence of a king. If he chose, he could rule a kingdom." Taking the hint and understanding that the Master wanted Rakhal to be their leader, Naren lost no time in bringing this about. One day, when all the young disciples were seated together, Naren spoke of Rakhal's greatness and announced: "From today, we shall call Rakhal our king." The others gladly agreed, knowing the special love which their master had for

Rakhal. Thus, from that day, they called him Raja, the king. Later on, both disciples and devotees began to call him "Maharaj." When Sri Ramakrishna heard Rakhal's new name, he joyfully approved.

He knew that his mission had been fulfilled, so, leaving his earthly body, he merged himself in the Divine Mother. On the 15th of August, 1886, the Master passed into *mahasamadhi*, the highest state of superconsciousness.

III

AS A YOUNG MONK

WHILE THE MASTER was still with them, the young disciples had lived in an atmosphere of continual joy and festivity. They were walking the path of God, who is infinite Being, infinite Wisdom, and infinite Bliss. They tasted the delight of their master's presence; and neither the anxieties of the world nor its pleasures and excitement could touch their hearts. "Live in union with Brahman and spread the joy of Brahman all around you." That was the truth that the disciples had learned.

In the Gospel according to St. Matthew (IX:15) we read: "And Jesus said unto them, Can the children of the bridechamber mourn, as long as the bridegroom is with them? but the days will come, when the bridegroom shall be taken from them, and then shall they fast."

Sri Ramakrishna was taken away from them and they felt a void, an emptiness. The Master had, as it were, lighted the candles within their hearts with a torch of blazing fire. Now that the torch had gone, they were conscious of darkness. Their own candles still burned; but they were not enough. They wanted the blazing torch. They wanted to be merged in that blissful consciousness once and forevermore.

Guided by an invisible hand, thirsting for God and fired with the ideal of renunciation, the young disciples gathered together and formed the Ramakrishna Monastic Order at Baranagore.

Naren was the center and heart of this group. Under his guidance the young disciples engaged themselves in study, discussion, and religious practices. Rakhal was put in charge of the monastery and made responsible for its general welfare. Naren and Rakhal loved and respected each other deeply. Once, a young member of the group felt discouraged and wished to leave. Rakhal said to him: "Why do you want to run away? There is such a wonderful atmosphere here. Where else would you find a holy man like Naren? And where else would you find such love as Naren has for us?"

Although some members of the new monastery had already received the gerua cloth from their master, they now followed Naren's suggestion and went through the formal ritual of *sannyas*—the taking of the monastic vow. Naren became known as Swami Vivekananda, and Rakhal as Swami Brahmananda.[1]

[1]These were the first monks of the Ramakrishna Order, the immediate disciples of Sri Ramakrishna:

The disciples now devoted themselves wholeheartedly to spiritual practices. Some days they had nothing to eat; and always their meals were scanty. Their only thought was of God, and in this thought they would remain absorbed almost continuously for days and nights on end.

In *The Gospel of Sri Ramakrishna*, "M." records the following conversation with Rakhal in the gardens of the Baranagore Monastery:

Rakhal: "Don't waste any more time. Plunge deep into spiritual practices.

"Why have we renounced the world? Some people say if you have failed to realize God, why not go back to the world? But Naren gives the right answer: 'Because we could not find Ram, must we live with

Naren	Swami Vivekananda
Rakhal	Swami Brahmananda
Baburam	Swami Premananda
Yogin	Swami Yogananda
Tarak	Swami Shivananda
Sarat	Swami Saradananda
Sashi	Swami Ramakrishnananda
Hari	Swami Turiyananda
Niranjan	Swami Niranjanananda
Latu	Swami Adbhutananda
Gangadhar	Swami Akhandananda
Sarada Prasanna	Swami Trigunatita
Kali	Swami Abhedananda
Gopal Sr.	Swami Advaitananda
Subodh	Swami Subodhananda

Another disciple of Sri Ramakrishna, Hari Prasanna, joined the monastic order some years later and became known as Swami Vijnanananda.

Shyam and beget children?"[1] Ah, Naren speaks wise words!"

M.: "What you say is true. I can see that you are filled with a great spiritual longing."

Rakhal: "How can I describe the state of my mind? This noon I felt a yearning to go to Narmada and practice austerity. Nothing can be achieved without diving deep into meditation. The outside world is full of distractions. Even Sukadeva, the pure and ever-free one, was afraid of the distractions of the world."

M.: "Yes, the Yogopanishad describes how Sukadeva renounced the world—the realm of maya. It also relates a conversation between Sukadeva and his father, Vyasa. Vyasa advises him to find God while living his life in the world. Sukadeva answers: 'The only truth is God.' He saw the emptiness of life in the world, the vanity of lust and greed."

Rakhal: "Many people mistakenly imagine that it is enough if one avoids the company of women, but Naren expressed the truth beautifully last night. He said: 'Woman exists for man as long as he has lust. When you are free from lust you do not see any difference between the sexes.'"

M.: "That is true. Children do not see the difference in sex."

Rakhal: "That is why I believe we must plunge deep within. To reach enlightenment a man must transcend maya, the domain of lust and greed."

[1]This means, if we cannot find God, do we have to be steeped in worldliness?

Most of the young disciples wanted to retire into complete solitude and live absorbed in God. The divine touch of their master had already enabled them to experience the transcendental state. What they had attained only now and then through his grace, they wished to win as a permanent possession by their own efforts. They wanted to live utterly in that consciousness. We find Swami Brahmananda eager to go into solitude, live on alms, and dwell constantly in union with Brahman.

Maharaj talked to Swamiji (as Vivekananda was usually called) about his intention of living for some time as a wandering monk, surrendering himself completely to God. Swamiji agreed, but suggested that Swami Subodhananda go with him and look after him. Because of his deep love for Maharaj, Swamiji was always concerned for his welfare, and wished him to have someone who would minister to his comforts. Maharaj could not refuse his brother's wish, so he and Swami Subodhananda left together for Benares. They stayed there a month. From Benares they went on to the temple of Omkarnath, situated on the bank of the river Narmada. Here, amidst charming natural surroundings, Maharaj lived continuously in *nirvikalpa samadhi* for six days and six nights, completely unconscious of the outside world. When at last he came back to normal consciousness, his face shone with a heavenly joy. He had experienced God in the impersonal, absolute aspect, and had realized the identity of the *Atman* with Brahman.

The two swamis continued their journey and reached Panchavati by the river Godavari where Sita and Rama are traditionally supposed to have lived during their exile. There is a temple dedicated to them. Here, Brahmananda felt and saw the living presence of these two divine incarnations; while chanting the Holy Name, he became absorbed in samadhi for three days and three nights.

During these periods, Swami Subodhananda used to watch over Maharaj with mingled joy and anxiety. He realized the danger that Maharaj might pass out of the body while in samadhi and not return to earthly life, and he was always careful to prevent this.

From Panchavati, they went on to Dwaraka, the well-known place of pilgrimage, situated on the bank of the sacred river Gomati. In this river pilgrims bathe in order to acquire merit, paying a tax for the privilege. But neither Maharaj nor Subodhananda had any money. A rich merchant noticed this and, recognizing them as holy men, offered to pay their tax, but Maharaj refused. He did not wish to buy religious merit and preferred to take his bath in the nearby ocean. This impressed the merchant so much that he also refused to pay the tax and went to bathe with the two swamis. He invited them to his residence and entertained them for three days, but when he offered them money for their further travels Maharaj refused to accept it. The merchant then offered to give them letters of introduction to his agents in different parts of the country so that their comfort would be assured wherever they went. But Maharaj refused this offer also. "I need nothing from anybody," he said. "The Lord is my only refuge! He will look after us." The merchant then gave him a copy of the Bhagavad-Gita, which was gladly accepted.

From Dwaraka they visited various places of pilgrimage and finally reached Brindaban. During this second visit to the holy city, Maharaj wrote Balaram the following letter:

"Who can fathom the workings of God? Who could know his divine play? Man remains subject to happiness and misery as long as he is bound by *karma.* This is the lot of every man—no matter whether he is learned or ignorant, good or wicked. Rare indeed is he who has attained unalloyed bliss! Only that man who is free from all cravings can find unending joy.

"There is more misery than happiness in this world. Most people live in misery. God the Father is loving and kind. Who can explain why his children suffer?

"Man suffers because of his ignorance. This ignorance is his sense of ego. When a man is free from this egoism, surrendering his life, his mind, and his intellect at the blessed feet of the Lord of all, renouncing all that he calls his own—then is he blessed indeed. That man alone is truly happy.

"Of himself, man can accomplish nothing. There is only one thing to be done: Pray to God and pray unceasingly. Thus we may forget the ego altogether and continually remember that God alone is real, that God alone is the Truth. Then only can we be freed from ignorance.

"Sri Ramakrishna used to say: 'How many love God as they love their own kith and kin? How many even want to love him?'

"The mind is created out of those three *gunas* which also make up the outer world. Because of this the mind finds delight in dwelling on worldly thoughts. This is the very nature and stuff of the mind. It is only through divine grace that a man can withdraw his mind from the external world and keep it fixed on God's holy feet.

"I pray to the Lord that I may be completely freed from consciousness of the physical world. Bless me, that I may remain absorbed in the Lotus Feet of the guru—that is the one desire of my heart."

Here in Brindaban, Brahmananda lived in a state of continuous ecstasy, almost entirely losing his consciousness of the physical world. His brother-disciple lovingly watched over him, but Brahmananda rarely spoke to him; his mind dwelt constantly in another realm. Subodhananda would beg food for him from door to door, and place it silently in a corner of his brother's cell. At a regular hour, Brahmananda would rise from meditation in order to eat something, but if Subodhananda was late and he did not find the food in the usual place, he did not mind. He simply returned to his meditation and ate nothing until the next day. Sometimes Subodhananda would collect a

rather more luxurious meal, with curries of various
kinds, but he noticed that Brahmananda satisfied his
hunger from one of the dishes and left the rest un-
touched. He did this not because he was deliberately
practicing any austerity or mortification of the flesh,
but because he was so completely absorbed in the
thought of God that the taste for food or any other
sense-object had left him. He ate only to keep the
body alive. In later years Maharaj used to say: "It is
easy to practice austerity by not allowing the mind to
come into contact with sense-objects, but it is hard to
get rid of the mental craving itself. And of all cravings
the subtle desire of the organ of taste is the most
difficult to overcome. A man loses this craving only
when he is in a high spiritual state."

Seeing Maharaj thus absorbed in contemplation
and neglecting food and sleep, Subodhananda one
day asked him: "Why do you live so strictly? You are
the spiritual son of God Incarnate; he has already
done everything for you. Through his grace you have
attained samadhi. Then why do you still have to sit
like a beggar, begging for the Lord's grace?"

"What you say is true," Maharaj answered. "The
Master did everything for us. But still I find a lack
within. This proves that we need repeated practice in
order to make the state of samadhi natural and
habitual to us. You know Uddhava was a devoted
disciple and friend of Sri Krishna; through his grace
he realized God. And yet Sri Krishna sent him to the
Himalayas to live in solitude and contemplation."

Bijoy Krishna Goswami, a well-known saint who was living in Brindaban at this time, asked Brahmananda the same question. He replied simply: "I am only trying to become established in that vision of God which I received through my master's grace." Bijoy Krishna and Maharaj would often meet and talk together about God.

In time, Subodhananda himself became eager to live in solitude and practice austerities. So, with the blessings and permission of Maharaj, he went to Hardwar at the foot of the Himalayas.

Left alone in Brindaban, Maharaj had no time to feel lonely, for again he plunged into the consciousness of God. Suddenly, one day, he saw in a vision the shining form of his devoted brother-disciple Balaram standing before him. On his face was a heavenly smile. Gradually his form merged into the light of the divine realm. Next day, Maharaj received the news that Balaram had passed away. At first he felt a pang of grief, for he loved Balaram dearly; then he realized that this sorrow also was a form of attachment. More strongly than ever he felt a desire to forget the things of the world and plunge deeper into the inner kingdom of God. He left Brindaban and began to walk toward Hardwar.

At Hardwar, Maharaj was overwhelmed by the grandeur and beauty of the Himalayas and of the Ganges running its course at their feet. Two miles from Hardwar is the quiet little village of Kankhal, sanctified by the presence of many monks belonging to various orders, who go there to lead contemplative lives. There Maharaj settled in a little hut not far from the Ganges. The present Ramakrishna Mission Home of Service is now situated on that very spot.

Swamis Vivekananda, Turiyananda, Saradananda, Subodhananda and other monastic disciples of the Master were then leading contemplative lives at Hrishikesh, in the same neighborhood. It was not long before they learned that Brahmananda was at Kankhal and they all went to visit him. Vivekananda wanted to go to Delhi and asked Maharaj and the rest of his brother-disciples to accompany him. Maharaj could not refuse any wish of Swamiji's, but first he wanted to visit Swami Akhandananda, another brother-disciple, who was living in Meerut. To Meerut, therefore, they all went and spent some memorable days in meditation and study, happy to be in one another's company. Then Swamiji left for Delhi alone; the rest of them followed later.

The lives of holy men, and especially their travels, must often appear curiously aimless to the ordinary observer. Ever obedient to the voice of God within them, they make no fixed plans as worldly people do. All their intentions are subject to unexpected change. No sooner were the swamis gathered in Delhi than Vivekananda told them that he must go on alone. The inner voice commanded him to seek solitude. "We shall meet again when the Lord wills," he told his brothers as he said good-bye.

Maharaj now asked Swami Turiyananda to accom-

pany him on his pilgrimage. The Swami readily
agreed, which pleased Maharaj very much, for Sri
Ramakrishna had once told him to "keep company
with Brother Hari."

In Hari (Turiyananda), devotion and knowledge
were harmoniously developed. Deeply learned in the
scriptures, he lived a life of great austerity and im-
maculate purity. Sri Ramakrishna used to speak of
him as a man of renunciation, strictly embodying the
ideal of the Gita.

The two swamis now traveled together, mostly on
foot, and visited many sacred temples in the northern
part of India. Turiyananda has told us that whenever
Maharaj entered any shrine he would be filled with
ecstatic devotion for that particular aspect of God to
which the temple was dedicated, and that, ultimately
he would have direct vision of the living deity within
that temple. In later years, when Maharaj was asked
by a disciple if the gods and goddesses are real, he
answered: "The one Godhead has many spiritual
forms. All these forms are real. A seer can see them
and talk to them."

After nearly two years of pilgrimage, the swamis
arrived in Bombay. There they met Kalipada Ghosh,
a devoted disciple of the Master, who lived in that
city. A joyful surprise awaited them, for at Kalipada's
house was Swamiji himself. Since the parting at
Delhi, they had known nothing of his whereabouts.
Swamiji was now preparing for his first journey to the
United States of America. Before embarking he was

requested to go and bless the newborn prince of Khe-tri. Brahmananda and Turiyananda went with him on the train as far as the Abu Road station. While Vivekananda was with the prince, they visited Mt. Abu, where there is a beautiful Jain temple. A few days later they returned to the station in time to exchange a few words with Swamiji as his train passed through. This meeting was very short. Swamiji hastily told Turiyananda: "Please go back to the Baranagore Monastery. You are wanted there. Let Raja live alone."

Turiyananda had no time to explain to Swamiji that he could not leave Maharaj alone just then. Brahmananda's spiritual consciousness was tuned so high that he had no regard for his body and could not look after it. So they remained together and the two of them returned to Mt. Abu, where they lived a life of contemplation. Turiyananda begged food for his brother and watched over him just as Subodhananda had done.

After some time, Maharaj felt that they should return to Brindaban. Here Turiyananda experienced a mood of ecstatic joy. "I am not going to beg any food today," he told Maharaj: "Let us see if Radha (the Holy Mother of Brindaban) will feed us." They sat down to meditate. Day and night passed for both in blissful absorption, without any consciousness of hunger or thirst. Next morning, as they rose from their meditation, they saw a devotee approaching them with quantities of food. By this time they were both hungry and ate with great relish.

After a few days in Brindaban, they went to Lake Kusum, a solitary place near the holy city. On the lake shore there are huts where monks can pass their days in solitude and contemplation. There the swamis lived for some months, completely forgetting the outer world.

Swami Turiyananda told me of an interesting experience Maharaj had at Lake Kusum. For several nights in succession, as he sat down to meditate, he was disturbed by peculiar noises and by the falling of pebbles and dust around him. At length Maharaj saw the spirit of a dead man standing before him. "Why are you disturbing me like this?" he asked. The spirit admitted that he had been trying to attract the Swami's attention, and begged Maharaj to liberate him from his pitiful condition. Maharaj replied that he did not know how to do this. "You are a holy man," the spirit told him: "If you will just pray for my release, I shall be liberated." Maharaj did as he was asked.

During his stay at Lake Kusum, Maharaj had the habit of rising at midnight and spending the rest of the night in meditation. One night, however, he felt tired and overslept. After a while, someone gave him a push and aroused him. At first he thought that this must be Swami Turiyananda; then he saw a luminous figure, in the dress of a Vaishnava saint, standing beside him and counting his beads. After this, the figure appeared almost every night, at midnight, and joined him in his meditation. Later, in describing this incident to his disciples, Maharaj remarked: "Many holy men, after leaving the physical body, live in subtle, spiritual bodies, and help earnest religious aspirants in different ways."

Toward the end of the year 1893, Turiyananda received a letter from a brother-disciple, describing Swamiji's success in America and requesting him to come back to the monastery, which had now been moved from Baranagore to Alambazar. Turiyananda read the contents of the letter to Maharaj and asked for his advice. Maharaj agreed that he ought to return. "Don't trouble about me," he said, "Go back to the monastery. You are needed there to do the work of the Lord."

So Turiyananda unwillingly took his departure, and Maharaj remained alone a year in Brindaban. During this period, he sometimes took a vow not to ask for food or other necessities of life from anyone. Generally an unknown devotee brought food to his door, but sometimes there would be days when he had nothing. Once, while he was sitting in silence, a stranger laid a warm new blanket beside him. A few moments later another stranger came by and took the blanket away. Maharaj sat still, smiling to himself as he watched the strange play of the Divine Mother.

During the special festivities in memory of Sri Krishna, Brahmananda joined the devotees at a nearby temple. The crowd was chanting the name of God and singing Krishna's praises before the shrine. An aged holy man of the Vaishnava sect was sitting in one corner, counting his beads. Suddenly he turned toward Maharaj and beckoned him to approach, indicating with affectionate gestures that he should sit down beside him. The two began to meditate; as Maharaj became absorbed, he felt the Vaishnava touch his head with his beads. He did this repeatedly, and each time, as Brahmananda received the saint's touch, the hair on his body stood on end and he experienced an ecstatic joy.

By constant practice throughout these years of pilgrimage, Maharaj had at last achieved his aim. The state of samadhi was now his own possession. He had won it for himself and he dwelt in it continually. Even in the periods of his normal consciousness, there was, as he said, "a fullness of God" in his heart. All around him, wherever he went, nature seemed to vibrate with joy. Established at last and forever in the consciousness of God, he felt ready to answer the call of worldly duty. One day, quite suddenly, he left for Calcutta, carrying that heavenly joy within his heart.

IV

PRESIDENT OF THE ORDER

THE RETURN OF MAHARAJ to Calcutta created a stir among his brother-disciples. His presence brought to them a new upsurge of spiritual joy. One day he told Swami Premananda: "I was very happy in Brindaban, but I left the holy city to come and live in the monastery here. I want to serve my brothers and mankind. Our master, Sri Ramakrishna, was the embodiment of supreme love and devotion; so that our own lives must be such that people all over the world, burdened by earthly sufferings and miseries, may learn to take his holy name and in him find rest and peace."

When Swamiji, who was still in America, heard of Brahmananda's return to Calcutta, he felt relieved of any further anxiety regarding the conduct of the Ramakrishna Order in India. His letters to Maharaj were full of the spirit of universal service; and Maharaj, in his turn, would inspire his brother-disciples with the same ideal. All felt an unbounded confidence in Swamiji and Maharaj; but the love of these two for each other was so deep and so spiritual that no one else could fully understand it. Two years after Brahmananda's return from Brindaban, Swamiji came back from America. A public reception was prepared for him at a house in Calcutta, and Maharaj himself was the first to welcome his brother, placing a garland of flowers around his neck. Swamiji, in his turn, touched the feet of Maharaj, quoting a saying from the scriptures: "The son of a guru is to be regarded as the guru himself," (meaning that Brahmananda was the spiritual son of Sri Ramakrishna). Smiling sweetly, Maharaj touched his feet and returned the compliment with another quotation: "One's elder brother is to be respected like one's father."

Swamiji was then taken to the Alambazar Monastery. Here he placed in Brahmananda's hands all the money which American devotees had subscribed toward the Indian Mission. "All this time," he said, "I have been acting as a trustee. It is a relief to give this back to its real owner—our Raja."

The natures of the two friends were widely dissimilar, and yet, in a sense, complementary. In the words of Sri Ramakrishna: "Naren dwells in the realm of the absolute, the impersonal. He is like a sharp, drawn sword of discrimination. Rakhal dwells in the realm of God, the Sweet One, the repository of all blessed qualities. He is like a child on the lap of his mother, completely surrendering himself to her in every way."

Vivekananda was like the flaming fire, the midday

sun—burning up all evil and impurity. Brahmananda was like a soft, cool light, soothing the aching heart. Vivekananda was like the deep and restless ocean— always fighting against ignorance and superstition. Brahmananda was like the blue sky, vast and patient in spirit. The manner of his working was inward and silent.

Vivekananda laid the foundation for the spiritual undertaking entrusted to him by his master. Brahmananda built the edifice. Vivekananda, with his dynamic, aggressive personality, could wake a man from the sleep of ignorance: Brahmananda with his characteristic serenity could show him the way to mold his life in God.

Each paid memorable tribute to the other. "Through Swamiji," said Brahmananda, "the world has come to know of Sri Ramakrishna. But for him, very few could have understood our master's genius." And in the words of Swamiji: "Raja is the greatest treasure house of spirituality." Once a European devotee came to visit Swamiji in the monastery, wishing to have his spiritual problems solved. Swamiji sent him to Maharaj, saying: "There you will find a dynamo working, and we are all under him." After talking to Maharaj, the devotee expressed his gratitude and told Swamiji that all his doubts had been removed.

Swami Saradananda rightly remarks: "If Swami Vivekananda was loved and cherished by the Master as the means by which his spiritual mission was to be proclaimed to the world, Swami Brahmananda was no less valued by him as the future head of his organization."

We have already described how, before visiting America, Swamiji had spent more than two years as a wandering monk, traveling the length and breadth of India. It was at this time that he came to understand the inner source of his country's strength, for he saw how the masses, in spite of their miserable poverty and lack of education, with all their accompanying evils, still held fast to the ancient ideals of religious life. Swamiji's heart thrilled with pride in his country's spiritual greatness, and bled for its material distress. When he came to the West, he found the picture exactly reversed. On the one hand, physical comfort, material prosperity, high standards of education, all the achievements of the human intellect; on the other hand, spiritual poverty, and a failure to understand life's only purpose—the unfoldment of the God within man. He saw, in short, that the West had failed to accept wholeheartedly the ideals of Jesus Christ. The perfect civilization, Swamiji realized, consists in blending and harmonizing the genius of the East with that of the West. Expressed philosophically, it is the blending of the active with the contemplative life.

When Swamiji returned to India, he talked to his brother-disciples, giving a new expression to the ideals for which Sri Ramakrishna had stood. It is not enough, he said, to devote your entire life to the realization of God for yourself alone. You must also live "for the good of all, for the happiness of all." Swamiji wished his brothers to combine the contemplative life with the life of service to mankind. Brahmananda was the first to recognize the depth and scope of Swamiji's ideals, and he gave them his full support.

On the first day of May 1897, Swamiji called a representative meeting of the monastic and lay disciples of Sri Ramakrishna. At this meeting, the organization known as the Ramakrishna Mission was formed. Maharaj was elected president of the Calcutta Center. Later, early in 1902, before the passing away of Swamiji, he was made head of the Order, and he held that office for more than twenty years, until his own death. The phenomenal growth of the Mission during his lifetime is too well known to need recording here. Whenever India has suffered any great flood or famine or other calamity, the monks of the Ramakrishna Order have come forward to relieve the distress of the people. Besides its innumerable emergency relief stations, opened temporarily, it has established permanent charitable and religious institutions all over the country. Preaching centers and monasteries have also been opened in Europe and in North and South America. At the beginning of 1899, the permanent headquarters of the Mission were established at Belur on the Ganges, now well known as the Belur Math.

Foreign visitors to India have spoken highly in

appreciation of the Mission's success in social service. To the monks of the Order, however, such success can be only of secondary importance. Maharaj always insisted on this: "The one purpose of life is to know God. Plunge deep into the sea of bliss and become immortals. Attain knowledge and devotion, then serve God in mankind. Work is not the end of life. Disinterested work is a means of attaining devotion. Meditate, meditate, and dive deep within. Know that God alone is real. Keep at least three-fourths of your mind in God. It is enough if you give one-fourth to service. Work and worship."

A young disciple of Swamiji, inspired by his ideals of renunciation and service, devoted himself to nursing the sick and helping the poor. From a very humble beginning, his work grew into a huge organization. For many years this disciple was the head of one of the largest homes of service in India under the Ramakrishna Mission. But when Maharaj saw that his work was becoming more important to him than his spiritual life, he relieved him of his post, inspired him with the ideal of realizing God, and sent him away to live a life of exclusive meditation.

To quote Maharaj again: "Yes, you must work. But I insist that you devote yourselves to spiritual practices and meditation. Even though I may not ask you to work, your nature will force you to work. It is difficult to engage the mind in contemplation of God; but you are monks, therefore work must not be the sole purpose of your lives."

At one time, a millionaire who had lost his wife came to the monastery and said he wished to renounce the world and give all his wealth to the Ramakrishna Mission. Swami Premananda reported this to Maharaj, who folded his hands and said gently: "Brother, a worldly man who associates with a holy man like yourself naturally becomes inspired by the ideal of renunciation. Shall we in our turn become worldly, because we have met a worldly man?" Maharaj refused to accept the money, because he knew very well that the millionaire would later regret his offer, being, as he was, very much attached to his wealth.

In the same way, he refused to accept a gift of real estate, knowing that the emotion which prompted the offer was merely temporary. He realized that the work of the Mission could not prosper unless it was founded on a firm spiritual basis.

Maharaj was more interested in the spiritual growth of his disciples than in their efficiency. He once reprimanded a senior disciple who had been put in charge of a younger brother, saying, "Did I send this young boy to you to make a good clerk out of him?" On another occasion, when a senior disciple of Swamiji was taking one of the younger disciples to task for negligence in some duty, Maharaj overheard the conversation and told him: "Of course, it is wrong if this young man neglects his allotted duty. You have the right to scold him for that. But tell me, do you ever inquire if he is doing his duty to himself? Do you

ask him if he is meditating regularly or if he has any
difficulties in his progress towards God? Is the work
of the Mission more important to you than this boy's
spiritual growth?"

Maharaj placed special importance on what he
called *sahaja yoga*, which means the easy way to
attain the knowledge of God. And that is constant
recollectedness. He used to say: "Make japam. Repeat the name of the Lord. Whatever you do, let the
name of God flow like a current within you."

While it is true that Maharaj held the ideal of
selfless service, of serving God in man, to be a form
of worship, he also pointed out that without the practice of meditation it is hard to do work as worship,
and that it is utterly impossible to annihilate the ego
simply by actions, however selfless they may be. We
must act but we must also try by our meditation to
merge the ego in God.

Jesus said: "Love thy neighbor as thyself." But to
really love mankind an aspirant must also learn to
love God with all his heart, his soul, and his mind.
Maharaj once told me: "My boy, devote yourself to
spiritual practices. Attain knowledge and devotion.
Then you will see how your heart will overflow with
love and sympathy for mankind. You will also find
out how unnecessary is man's suffering, carrying as
he does this mine of bliss within himself."

MAHARAJ KEPT A WATCHFUL EYE on the progress
of each member of the Order. He turned our hearts

continually toward God and directed our actions and the activities of the Mission toward the integrating of that inner strength which alone can benefit mankind physically, morally, and spiritually.

When young men of varied temperaments live together, it is only natural that misunderstandings will arise from time to time, no matter how high their common ideal may be. In one of the monasteries, connected with a home of service, there were a number of young untrained members, newly arrived from school and college. When they had been together a while, their old tendencies began to reassert themselves: they formed rival groups and started to quarrel. A senior swami of the Order went to investigate. After questioning everybody he soon found out who were the ringleaders. He then wrote to Swami Brahmananda telling him that some of those boys were unfit for monastic life, and should be expelled. Maharaj replied: "Don't do anything. I am coming to see for myself."

When Maharaj arrived, he asked no questions. He lived quietly in the monastery, insisting only on one thing: that all the boys should meditate regularly in his presence. Then he began to instruct them, making no distinction between the good and the bad. Gradually the whole atmosphere of the place improved. The boys forgot their quarrels because they no longer had any time for them. And when Maharaj left, two or three months later, perfect harmony had been restored in the monastery. Nobody had been expelled.

All the boys had become better and more spiritual.

At another time, two young monks quarreled and came to blows. Swami Premananda heard of it and went anxiously to Maharaj, saying: "Maharaj, we brother-disciples have lived together in peace and harmony for many years. Never have we fought or quarreled; never has a harsh word been spoken among us. What shall we do with these boys? Ought we not to expel them?"

"Brother," Swami Brahmananda answered gently, "it is true that they have been making trouble, but remember also that they came here to take refuge at the blessed feet of Sri Ramakrishna. They look to you for counsel and guidance. Surely you can do something to transform their lives and bring love into their hearts."

"You are right," Swami Premananda replied, "they have taken refuge here; but, brother, it is you who must bless them and transform them."

Then Swami Premananda gathered the monks together, seniors and novices alike, and led them in procession to Maharaj. With folded hands the Swami asked Maharaj to bless them all. As he spoke, Maharaj entered into an exalted spiritual mood. He became deeply absorbed, and his right hand was raised in benediction.

Seeing this, Swami Premananda asked Swami Shuddhananda, a senior disciple of Swamiji, to prostrate before Maharaj and receive his blessing. Thereupon, every monk and every initiate followed his example, and Maharaj touched the head of each with his uplifted hand. Speaking from my own experience, I can only say that that touch was like a cooling spring to a fevered body. It gave one an inner exaltation which could be felt but not described. All our troubles were forgotten and our hearts were full of love.

"Keep your mind as high as the mountains," Maharaj told a disciple whom he was sending to a monastery in the Himalayas. He himself lived always in an exalted state of consciousness, which subtly transformed the lives and characters of those around him. If the spiritual life is intensified, the outer life will adjust itself automatically; this principle applies equally to the life of an organization. Maharaj was once asked to make some new rules for the guidance of the young monks. He replied: "Swamiji has already made our rules for us. We do not need to add any new ones. Add more love, attain more devotion, and help others to move toward the ideal of God."

As the network of monasteries and homes of service spread over India, Maharaj began to visit them, staying a few months at each place. He inspired everyone by his presence, and an air of festivity prevailed everywhere he went. Once, in speaking of him, Swami Turiyananda quoted a verse from the Bhagavatam: "Those who realize the eternal presence of the Lord in their hearts are endowed with goodness and beauty, and their lives are a perpetual festival of joy." Then he added: "Maharaj carries with him such an intense spiritual atmosphere that whoever comes within his orbit is carried toward God as if by a spiritual current and is filled with divine joy." Once a professor who had lived for a week in the monastery which Maharaj was visiting said to me: "I don't know what kind of boys you are, but if you can live in the rarefied atmosphere of Maharaj, day after day, you must be great. I myself cannot stand it for long; I need to breathe a little worldly air." However, after this, the professor could not breathe his worldly air for long. Maharaj had given him a taste of the joy of God. Soon afterward he came back and joined the Order.

Though Maharaj could not be in all the centers at once or live with all his disciples, he kept a watchful eye on everybody. One day he said to me: "Do you think I don't know what you boys have been doing and how you have been faring in the path to God? I may stay in one place and seem unconcerned, but I know what is happening to each one of you. I even know what . . . is doing in America." Maharaj possessed this knowledge not through the ordinary means of communication, but through extraordinary powers. Moreover, he was not satisfied with merely knowing: he sent spiritual aid to everyone in need.

If a member of the Order should be guilty of some serious offense and there would be talk of his expulsion, Maharaj would forgive his misdeeds and transform him by his touch. He used to say: "The sins of many births can be wiped out in a moment by one glance from the gracious eye of God." Once he said to me: "What is morality? If one acquires devotion to God, morality and purity will follow without one even trying to be moral or pure."

"Practice, practice," he would tell us: "Through practice of the spiritual disciplines the heart will be purified and a new realm will open. You will realize that God alone is real and that everything else is unreal. But when through japam and meditation a little awakening comes, do not imagine you have achieved the end. Light! More Light! Onward! Onward! Attain God! Gain his vision! Talk to him!"

The success of a religious body depends, not on its external achievements, its efficient organization, its buildings, the size of its membership or its philanthropic activities—but upon the inner life of each of its members and the measure of their progress toward devotion and knowledge of God. This is the truth that Maharaj, as head of the Order, impressed indelibly upon our minds.

V

MAHARAJ AS GURU

SRI RAMAKRISHNA ONCE SAID: "When the lotus blooms, bees come of their own accord to gather the honey. When the lotus of a man's heart blossoms in the joy of God, spiritual aspirants will swarm to him." Many times we have watched Maharaj sitting among a crowd of devotees. One moment, he would be as happy and playful as a child; then suddenly his mind would become indrawn and the whole atmosphere would vibrate with the presence of God. At such times, those who had come to visit him would find that all their doubts and problems had been solved. They would rise and leave his presence, exalted and comforted, though not a single word had been spoken.

The monastic order included many disciples of Holy Mother and Swamiji. But most of these had little opportunity of associating with their gurus. Swamiji passed away in 1902, and because Holy Mother did not live at the monastery she instructed her disciples to follow the disciplines prescribed by Maharaj. Maharaj himself also accepted disciples, but at first he was very particular. Often he would initiate them only after many years of probation. During the ceremony of initiation, he would be filled with an ecstasy of love, and the disciple would feel an extraordinary sense of the divine presence.

Holy Mother once complained that Maharaj did not accept enough disciples. It so happened that just then Maharaj was invited to see a play about the life of Ramanuja, which had been written by one of his own disciples. In this drama there is a scene which expresses Ramanuja's great love for mankind. The action is as follows:

Ramanuja's guru initiates him with a sacred mantram, and warns him never to reveal it to anyone. "What will happen if I do?" Ramanuja asks. And his guru replies: "Whoever hears this mantram will be liberated from the bondage of his ignorance, but you yourself will suffer damnation." Ramanuja goes at once into the temple, gathers a crowd around him, and utters the sacred mantram in the hearing of all. His guru pretends to be very angry, and rebukes him for his disobedience. Ramanuja answers: "If my damnation can liberate so many people, then my supreme desire is to be damned." The guru is delighted. "You are great indeed!" he exclaims. "I give you my blessing." And he declares that the philosophy of qualified monism is to be known in the future as the Ramanuja philosophy.

This drama and Holy Mother's remark both made a deep impression upon Maharaj. After this, he initiated many more disciples.

Maharaj recognized his future disciples at first sight, and bound them to him at once with an indescribable love. Even as he met them, he knew which spiritual path each should follow. Two young college boys came to visit him. To one of them, he said jokingly: "Let me see your palm." As he looked at it, he remarked: "You have a tendency toward worldly enjoyments. But, by the Lord's grace, you may be able to overcome it." Swami Premananda, who was present, asked Maharaj to look at the other boy's hand also. He replied, smiling: "I don't need to." Hearing this, the other boy (who was later to be known as Swami Yatiswarananda) felt sad. He thought: "My friend has some chance of becoming a monk, but I have none." A few days later, he came alone to visit Maharaj at the Belur Monastery. He met Swami Brahmananda's personal attendant, who told him: "Maharaj said that you would become a monk." And indeed, he did; a few years later he became a monk, while the other boy married but remained a devotee.

Before Yatiswarananda became a monk, Maharaj told him: "Give your body and mind to worldly enjoyments, and the world will destroy them both. Devote them to God and his service, and you will enjoy bodily health, peace of mind, and spiritual joy."

The following is Yatiswarananda's own description of his initiation: "The day Maharaj was to initiate me, I felt a spiritual power tangibly emanating from him. After the initiation, I bowed down to him. He raised his hand in benediction above my head, giving me instantly a vivid consciousness of an immanent Presence. I realized that the whole universe was merged in that Presence. That day, also, I got a glimpse of the divine nature and power of the guru. I was literally transported into a new life, and the power that he transmitted to me that day is still working within me."

There are some instances of persons receiving initiation from Maharaj in dream. This has happened even when the dreamer had never seen him in the flesh, but had merely heard about him and felt attracted by his name. One devout young woman had such a dream, and went to see Maharaj to confirm it. Although he was seated among his brother-disciples, she recognized Maharaj at first sight, and began to describe her experience. Just as she was about to repeat the mantram she had received in her dream, Maharaj stopped her. "Don't tell me," he said, "I will tell you what it was." Thus she was convinced of the truth of her vision.

A young boy also received a mantram from Maharaj in a dream, but unfortunately forgot it when he awoke. Shortly afterward, he went to Maharaj for initiation. During the ceremony, the dream-mantram returned to his mind, so that he was delighted and surprised when, a few moments later, Maharaj gave him that very same mantram.

At one time Sri Ramakrishna appeared in a dream to two ladies belonging to an aristocratic family, and told them to visit Maharaj. They had never heard of Sri Ramakrishna, nor read anything about him. But they went to Maharaj and were initiated by him. After relating this incident, Maharaj remarked to me: "You see, we think we have to preach the Lord and his message; but Sri Ramakrishna does his own preaching. Be the witness!"

Girish Chandra Ghosh, the famous Bengali dramatist who became a disciple of Sri Ramakrishna, tells the following story about Brahmananda's extraordinary power: "Compared to myself, Rakhal is only a young lad. I know that Sri Ramakrishna regarded him as his spiritual son, but that is not the only reason why I feel such a deep reverence for him. Once, while I was seriously ill, I found that I had lost my faith in Sri Ramakrishna. My heart felt dry. Many of the brother-disciples came to see me, and I told them about the unhappy state of my mind, but they only kept silent. Then, one day, Rakhal came. He asked me how I felt, and I described the dryness and lack of devotion from which I was suffering. Rakhal listened attentively, then he laughed aloud. 'Why worry about it?' he asked me. 'The waves of the ocean rise high, then they go down again, and again they rise. The mind is like that. But please do not be troubled. Your present mood is due to the fact that you are about to rise to a much higher level of spirituality. The wave of the mind is gathering strength.' When he left me, all the dryness in my heart had gone. My faith had returned, and my mind rose to a higher level than ever before."

Maharaj initiated me while I was still a college student of eighteen. I wanted to join the monastery at that time but Maharaj instructed me to finish my education first. While at the university, I became involved with the revolutionary movement to overthrow the English government. However I did not lose my interest in spiritual life. In 1914, during Christmas vacation, I stayed a few days at the Belur Monastery in order to study Vedanta philosophy—one of my courses at the university—with Swami Shuddhananda, a disciple of Swami Vivekananda and a great and learned scholar of Hindu philosophy. He used to urge me to become a monk. But I would argue with him: I thought the monastic life was lazy. I wanted to devote myself to political activities, believing that India must be freed from the domination of the British. An old man, who was also a guest at the monastery, used to be present during these arguments. Swami Shuddhananda could never convince me. One morning, as usual, I went to prostrate before Maharaj. This old man was also in the room. Suddenly he asked Maharaj: "When is this boy going to become a monk?" Maharaj looked me up and down, and his eyes had an unforgettable sweetness as he answered quietly: "When the Lord wills." That was the end of my political plans and ambitions. I remained at the monastery.

My own case was not exceptional. Many politically-minded young men who came into contact with Maharaj were inspired by the spiritual ideals of renunciation, service, and of realizing God. They began to realize that the awakening of India would never come through political action, but only through an intensification of the nation's spiritual life—and that this awakening would benefit not India merely but all mankind.

Maharaj had wonderful insight into the character and spiritual growth of individuals. A friend of mine, whom he knew, renounced the world and went to Hrishikesh to practice austerity. He would not accept the guidance of any guru. After a few months' practice he wrote me, saying that he had attained samadhi. At that time I was with Maharaj at Kankhal, and I told him the substance of my friend's letter.

"Why!" exclaimed Maharaj: "I saw him about ten days ago. I looked into his eyes. He has not had samadhi. No doubt, he has had some kind of mystic vision—the vision of light, perhaps—and he mistakes that for samadhi. An aspirant is often led astray like that, when he has no guru to advise him.

"Samadhi! Is it an easy matter to attain samadhi? We saw Swamiji in samadhi only a few times. Sri Ramakrishna alone we saw in samadhi many times each day and night."

Then he quoted a verse from the Mundaka Upanishad: "The knot of the heart, which is ignorance, is loosed, all doubts are dissolved, all evil effects of deeds are destroyed, when he who is both personal and impersonal is realized."

"Is it ever possible," I asked, "to attain samadhi after a short time?"

"Yes, if a man has lived an absolutely continent life."

ONCE I TOLD MAHARAJ about a swami who had been stung by a scorpion and seemed to be miraculously cured by the power of a mantram. Maharaj laughed and said: "Come along!" He took me to the garden, pointed to a plant, and told me: "Look, the juice of this plant cures a scorpion sting!"

Maharaj did not want his disciples to be credulous or superstitious. By his attitude he taught me to rely upon natural explanations rather than look for supernatural phenomena.

MAHARAJ, WITH HIS DEEP INSIGHT, knew the strength and weakness of each of his disciples. He was always ready to help, but insisted that the disciples should also make some effort. Once, I asked him to free my mind from lust. "I could do that for you," he replied, "but then, my child, you would lose all the joy of struggle. Life would seem insipid."

One morning, Swami Gnaneshwarananda hurried out of his room, leaving behind an unmade bed and general confusion. He met Maharaj on the *maidan*, a large, open field near his room. After paying his respects, he was startled to hear Maharaj say: "Take me to your room; I wish to see the place where you sleep."

Swami Gnaneshwarananda, feeling ashamed, replied: "Maharaj, can you not come a little later? I was not expecting you and the room is not fit to receive you."

Maharaj said: "My boy, you must always be expecting me."

Swami Gnaneshwarananda understood the deep meaning of the incident and words of Maharaj—that one must always be prepared to receive the Lord, the most honored guest.

Sri Ramakrishna himself often rebuked his most intimate disciples, and Maharaj also used this method to train those who were near and dear to him. The chastening of a disciple never began, however, until after he had enjoyed several years of love and kind words. These experiences were painful at the time, but they were later treasured among the disciple's sweetest memories. It often happened that even while the disciple was being reproached by Maharaj, he would feel a strange undercurrent of joy. The indifference of Maharaj was the only thing we could not have borne; but Maharaj was never indifferent. The harsher his words, the more intensely we felt his interest in our welfare. The very fact that he could speak to us in this way proved that we were his children, his own. Sometimes, a disciple would be reproved for quite insignificant reasons, or on grounds that seemed to him utterly unjust. But, as time passed, he would realize that there had been certain tendencies and karmas stored in his subconscious mind, and that Maharaj had seen them and was working to annihilate them before they could appear and become harmful. Thus, at the cost of a little unpleasantness, the disciple would be spared years of painful struggle and self-discipline.

At one time Maharaj was disciplining me continually. All day long he would scold me. On one occasion I was supposed to have some stationery designed for him. I examined the proofs of the letterheads carefully before I presented several ornamental fonts to him from which to choose. When the stationery was printed, one of my brother-disciples took it to Maharaj, and then came back trembling: "Maharaj says the 'S' is broken!" I went to Maharaj. He scolded me vehemently. Then I opened the stylebook and showed him that the space in the letter "S" to which he was objecting was really a part of the design. Nevertheless, he continued to scold me.

Although he did not mention the real reason for his scolding, he somehow gave me to understand that it had nothing to do with the letterheads—the apparent cause of his rebuke. He was wiping out karmas from my subconscious mind.

When Maharaj disciplined us, he gave us the power to bear it. We never reacted with resentment. We knew that whatever he did was for our own good.

There was only one occasion when I felt that I had perhaps lost my master's love, and because I could not endure the thought, that very night I decided to run away from the monastery and hide myself forever. Thus resolved, I went next morning to prostrate before Maharaj, and silently take my leave of him. I was about to go, when he told me to sit down. For a while he continued to scold me, reminding me of all my faults. Then with a sudden change of manner and great earnestness, he asked: "Do you think you can run away from me? The mother holds the child on her lap and spanks him; and the child cries: 'Mother, mother!' " Never before had I been so deeply aware of his love and protection. All thought of running away was forgotten. His words soothed my burning heart. Then he said: "Our love is so deep that we do not let you know how much we love you."

The truth of this statement was proved to me as I watched how Maharaj dealt with Hariharananda, another disciple who had been for many years his personal attendant. Hariharananda had begun to depend too much upon our master; he needed to learn to stand on his own feet. So, with a show of displeasure, Maharaj sent him away to practice austerities in the solitude of a temple in Southern India. Some years later, Maharaj was in Madras and arranged for Hariharananda to visit him. I was alone with Maharaj throughout the entire evening on which he was to arrive. Watching Maharaj, I saw that he was as rest-

less as a loving mother who was expecting her son
after a long absence. In due time, Hariharananda arrived, but, fearing that Maharaj was still angry with
him, he felt shy and wanted to postpone their meeting
until the morning. Knowing the real state of affairs,
I insisted that he should see Maharaj at once. However, when Hariharananda came into the room,
Maharaj no longer showed any sign of his loving
anxiety. He merely greeted his disciple quietly and
asked if he had been keeping well.

On another occasion, while I was being reproved
in the presence of Ramlal Dada, the nephew of Sri
Ramakrishna, another young disciple entered the
room. Maharaj turned to him and said jokingly:
"With those glasses on, you look like Keshab Sen."
The disciple did not answer, for he saw that I was
being scolded. Then Ramlal Dada turned to him and
said: "Do you know why Maharaj is rebuking this
boy in your presence? There is a saying that the
mother scolds her daughter in order to teach the
daughter-in-law."

I remember the first time Maharaj ever reproved
me. I had failed to do a certain errand for him, because I had not understood exactly what it was he
wanted. For this neglect he scolded me throughout
the afternoon. At supper time, Swami Turiyananda
was seated with Maharaj and I was fanning them. The
scolding continued. I remained silent. Swami Turiyananda turned to me and asked: "Do you know why
Maharaj is so hard on you?"

"No," I replied, "frankly, I don't. I do not see how I am to blame."

Then Swami Turiyananda said: "There are three classes of disciples. The third-class disciple merely does the guru's bidding. The second-class disciple does not have to be told. He acts as soon as the thought arises in the guru's mind. But the first-class disciple acts even before the guru has had time to think. Maharaj wants you all to become first-class disciples."

To this Maharaj added simply: "You see, brother Hari, I am getting old; they do not obey me any more. Please knock a little sense into their heads."

There was another time when I did not write to Maharaj because my vanity had been wounded. When he came to Madras from Bangalore and asked me why I had not written, I answered carelessly: "Oh, you got all news of me from Swami Shivananda."

At a glance, he understood my mood, and asked sarcastically: "I suppose you have the key to the treasure house inside you, and don't need me any more?" My ill humor vanished immediately. "How can you say that?" I exclaimed: "You know that you hold the key!"

Maharaj continued to scold me for my negligence in not writing to him. Then he told me how Sri Ramakrishna, by his mere touch, removed the spiritual obstacles that stood in his disciple's path. To this I answered: "Yes—Sri Ramakrishna did all that for you. But when our turn comes you can only scold us."

Maharaj shook his head, and said with great sweetness: "No, my boy. You have no need to worry." Then he repeated three times: "I see how Sri Ramakrishna is doing everything for you."

Even though Maharaj once said: "Our love is so deep that we do not let you know how much we love you," there is still the fact that you can get honey from a honeycomb if you poke it. He could not always hide his deep love and concern. This was made evident to me when at one time I asked permission to live in solitude and practice austerities.

At first he granted my request, but I did not realize then that he was not really serious. He had said: "All right, go to the River Narmada and practice austerities, and let me see what you can do!"

Within a few weeks I had made the necessary arrangements—and my blanket and clothing were packed and ready. When I came to bid Maharaj goodbye and receive his blessings, he asked with alarm: "Where are you going?" I replied: "You have given me permission to go to the Narmada and practice austerities. I am ready to go."

Like a father about to lose his only son, he anxiously requested that I call Swami Snivananda at once. The Swami came immediately. As if he himself could not convince me that I should stay, Maharaj explained the situation to Swami Shivananda. With some agitation, he said: "Look, brother, this boy wants to practice austerities! What do these boys know about such things? Why do they have to practice austerities? We have done all that for them."

After this Maharaj began to speak of high spiritual matters. Other monks of the Order gathered. He continued to talk in this way for three hours, stopping only when he was told that a householder devotee wanted to see him. He remarked: "Now I can't continue. My mind has come down to a lower level." Later, Swami Shivananda said to me: "Today I learned many things I had not known before—just because you poked the honeycomb of Maharaj."

Sometimes the harsh behavior of Maharaj toward a disciple amounted to apparent cruelty. Three of us were to be initiated into the monastic order at the same time. One was a boy who had been greatly praised because he had steadfastly practiced spiritual disciplines. We had all noticed his growth. Just as the formal rites were about to begin, Maharaj suddenly turned to this boy and said: "Why are you here? I shall not initiate you. Go away."

My brother-disciple and I were both shocked and felt that Maharaj had been cruel. But the boy himself later admitted that the praise he had received had made him vain. Maharaj, by his drastic action, had killed the seed which might have grown into deadly spiritual pride. For ten days he suffered bitterly. Then he also was initiated into sannyas.

Maharaj also taught by joking and making fun. Often his humorous remarks contained a deep inner meaning. To one disciple he used to write doggerel verses, and the truths they expressed were sometimes far from pleasant. While in Madras, he used to dictate these poems to me. One of them had a line in it: "I have given that which is holy unto a dog." He told me to mail this poem to the disciple. Its harshness pained me and I spoke of it to Ramlal Dada, saying that I was afraid the feelings of the disciple would be deeply hurt. Ramlal Dada reported my remark to Maharaj. Meanwhile, I had gone to bed, but Maharaj sent for me. He told me to bring the poem and read it to him. I did so, and repeated my objection. Maharaj was silent for a moment. Then he said: "No, send it as it is. He is too thick-skinned to get my meaning any other way." And how right he was! These verses made a deep impression upon the disciple and awakened his spiritual understanding.

The reproaches of Maharaj were always followed by tenderness and sweetness. About a week before Maharaj left Madras I was arranging flowers in his room. I did not notice that he had come in. Suddenly he whispered into my ear: "Lovest thou me?" A thrill passed through my whole being, and for a moment I could neither speak nor move. When I was able to turn around, I saw that he was already leaving the room.

I still remember the last words Maharaj ever spoke to me. It was on the eve of his departure from Madras; I was cooking a sweet for him and he was walking up and down, close by. Suddenly, he came over and whispered into my ear: "It makes me feel so bad, having to leave you. I shall miss you very much." Later, at the end of a letter, he repeated those same loving words: "I miss you very much."

"M." ONCE TOLD Vishwananda, a disciple of Maharaj: "Observe how Maharaj acts and you will have some idea of what Sri Ramakrishna was like. When his mind came down to the finite plane, his sense of humor was very keen." This was also true of Maharaj. One of his favorite jokes was to have some fruits or sweets placed beside a disciple who was meditating. When the disciple had finished his meditation he would find his favorite dishes laid out before him. Later Maharaj would ask: "Well, did you get the fruits of your austerities?"

Often he would make us all roar with laughter. I remember once, while we were laughing, he nudged me and said, pointing to Vishwananda: "Look! How he giggles like a girl!" Maharaj would sometimes remark: "It is good to laugh every day. It relaxes the body and the mind."

The following stories will give a glimpse of Maharaj's sense of fun, and also of the deep love he bore toward his brother-disciples. One story is told by Swami Satprakashananda:

ONE AFTERNOON MAHARAJ was seated on the large bench on the ground-floor veranda of the Math build-

ing facing the Ganges. The old Math building pro-
vided the only residential quarters of the Belur monastery at that time.

I was standing very close to Maharaj. Presently, a
young man, who had come to the monastery to spend
a vacation in the company of holy men, approached
Maharaj to take leave of him. His holiday was over,
and he was about to return to his own home.

Maharaj had noticed that, during his stay, the
young man had been particularly devoted to Swami
Premananda, who was the center of attraction to
many ardent visitors in those days.

With his characteristic sense of humor, Maharaj
took the opportunity to have a little fun at the expense of his brother-disciple, Swami Premananda.

"Have you taken leave of Swami Premananda?" he
asked as the young man bowed down before him.
"No, Maharaj, not yet," he replied; "I am going to
take leave of him now."

"Well, when you bow down to him you should say
the *pranama-mantra* (salutation mantra). Perhaps
you do not know this mantram, but I shall teach
you!"

So saying, Maharaj began to recite a Bengali couplet which he improvised as he went along. Freely
translated, it ran something like this: "My mind is
reluctant to go back home; it is my heart's desire to
lie down forever at those blessed feet."

Then Maharaj instructed him how to act while
saying the mantram. He told him to first stand before

Swami Premananda with hands folded in great veneration, and repeat the couplet until he came to the line "to lie down forever at those blessed feet," when he was to direct his still folded hands toward the Swami's feet, and then dive down.

The young man turned to go, and as he left, Maharaj told me to go and watch. I followed the youth and saw him standing before Swami Premananda with folded hands as Maharaj had instructed him. But he was silent. However, as he bowed down, the Swami noticed that he was mumbling something, and asked: "What is this? What are you saying? Speak out, my boy!" But the boy remained silent. And then I laughed. Hearing me laugh, Swami Premananda turned to me and said: "Ah! You know what he is saying, surely! Please tell me!" And then I told him the whole story of the pranama-mantra, and when I had finished there was a roar of laughter.

THE OTHER STORY tells of an affectionate trick Maharaj played on his brother-disciple, Swami Akhandananda. The Swami had been staying with Maharaj for some considerable time, when he decided he would like to return to his own *ashrama*. Maharaj begged him to stay a little while longer, but the Swami persisted.

Seeing his evident determination to go, Maharaj engaged a palanquin to take the Swami to the railway station, which was several miles away. The train was due in the early morning, which meant that the Swami had to leave late at night.

Before the bearers set out with Swami Akhandananda, Maharaj whispered something to them. It was dark when they left, so the Swami settled down behind the curtains of the palanquin. Every once in a while the bearers would stop, and the Swami would anxiously inquire what they were stopping for. Each time, they assured him that they were stopping merely to rest and to have a smoke, but that there was no need for anxiety; he would arrive at his destination in plenty of time.

After several hours of arduous travel the bearers finally stopped for the last time, and asked Swami Akhandananda to alight. Just as he was about to get out of the palanquin he saw Maharaj standing before him, greeting him as though he had just arrived after a long absence. When the Swami realized that he had been carried around the compound all night he roared with laughter. Maharaj embraced him and they both laughed like two children.

THE RELATIONSHIP between guru and disciple, according to the Hindu scriptures, is a very sacred one. Maharaj used to say that an enlightened soul must help his disciple until he also becomes enlightened. This tie cannot be broken by the death of the body. After the teacher has passed away, he still continues to watch over his disciples in spirit. He will not accept his own final liberation until all are liberated.

Maharaj was the embodiment of the protective power of the guru. At one time, he was walking with another disciple and myself. He was slightly ahead of us. Suddenly we heard a shout: "Out of the way! There's a mad bull!" An instant later, we saw the bull itself, rushing toward us. There was no time to run. My brother-disciple and I tried to get in front of Maharaj to protect him, but he raised his arms and pushed us back. Although he was now an elderly man, he was still extraordinarily strong. As the bull approached with lowered head, there was a moment's pause; Maharaj stood still, confronting it. Then the bull stopped, shook its head from side to side, lifted it, and walked quietly away.

Swami Akhilananda relates a similar incident which took place at Bhubaneswar. Maharaj had gone for an evening walk in the woods with Akhilananda and another devotee. By the time they turned homeward, it was dark. All at once they saw a leopard coming toward them. Maharaj stood still. The leopard also stopped, about a hundred feet away, and looked at them for some moments. Then it turned and ran off. Neither of the devotees felt frightened. There could never be any fear in the presence of Maharaj.

Maharaj prescribed various disciplines and diverse forms of worship to suit the different temperaments of his disciples. He knew our needs far better than we did. When I first joined the Order I was inclined toward the path of devotion, but Maharaj decided to send me to a monastery in the Himalayas where the ideal of nondualism is practiced and no ritual is allowed. Before I left, he made me read aloud to him a book on extreme nondualism. Two years later, he sent me to the monastery in Madras where ritual is regarded as very important. By this time I had lost all my devotional inclination and no longer believed in ritualistic worship. Some time later, Maharaj came to visit this monastery. One day, a devotee brought a large basket of *naga lingam* flowers to be offered in the worship. Knowing that they were the favorite flowers of Maharaj, I arranged them in his room. Maharaj came in, saw what I was doing, and asked: "Have you saved some of those flowers for the worship of the Lord?"

"No, Maharaj," I replied. For I had thought to myself: "After all, the Lord in the shrine room is only a picture, but the guru is the living God." Maharaj, as usual, read my thoughts, and asked: "Do you think it is merely a picture that is worshiped in the shrine?"

"Yes," I replied, somewhat nervously.

"Have you ever performed the ritualistic worship?"

"No, Maharaj."

"Why not?"

"I am not yet a swami, and I am not a *brahmin* by caste. So I am not allowed to do the external worship in the shrine."

Maharaj became quite excited. "What is all this?" he exclaimed. "Call Sharvananda."

Swami Sharvananda was a disciple of Maharaj and the head of the Madras monastery. When he appeared, Maharaj asked him: "How is it that a *brahmachari* of this Order is not allowed to do the worship, just because he is not a brahmin?"

Sharvananda answered: "Swami Ramakrishnananda was the first head of this monastery. He was very particular that the worship should be performed only by a swami or a brahmin."

"It should not be that way," Maharaj replied. "Anyone who has been initiated and who has entered the Order is purified in his body and birth; therefore, he should be allowed to do the worship." Then, turning to me, he said: "You will do the worship."

"But Maharaj," I replied, "I do not believe in ritualistic worship. I do not see the living Presence in the picture."

"I am asking you to do the worship now," Maharaj said quietly. "Will you?"

I obediently followed his instructions and, within a few days, became convinced of the great efficacy of external worship.

Almost his last advice to me was: "Be ritualistic." And he added: "Look at Ambikananda (one of his senior disciples); see how wonderfully he is progressing through the practice of ritualism."

This does not mean, however, that Maharaj asked everybody to practice ritualism. In fact, there are many of his disciples who have never learned the rites of formal worship. Hinduism teaches the value of ritual, but does not say that it is essential to everyone's spiritual progress.

I must mention two quotations which Maharaj never tired of repeating to his disciples. The first was: "Tell the truth, but never a harsh truth." The second was from the teachings of Sri Chaitanya:

> Be humbler than a blade of grass,
> Be patient and forbearing like the tree,
> Take no honor to thyself,
> Give honor to all,
> Chant unceasingly the Name of the Lord.

I will conclude this chapter by giving an example of the way in which the guru power of Maharaj was manifested. Swami Vivekananda once remarked: "A real guru knows the past, present, and future of all his disciples." Maharaj knew this about each one of us, as is shown by the following incident which a monastic disciple describes:

"I was sitting cross-legged in front of Maharaj with his feet resting on my knees. This was the position in which I often used to massage his feet. Then something happened to me which I cannot explain, though I feel certain that it was Maharaj's doing. I found myself in a condition in which I was talking and talking, forgetting my usual restraint; it seemed to me that I spoke freely and even eloquently for a long time, but I do not remember what I said. Maharaj listened and said nothing.

"Suddenly I returned to normal consciousness and became aware of Maharaj leaning toward me and asking with an amused smile: 'What did you say?' I then realized that I had addressed him as 'tumi' (the familiar form of 'you' which is used in speaking to equals and friends). I hastened to correct myself, repeating the sentence—I have forgotten what it was— but using 'apani' (the respectful form of 'you' by which we addressed him). At this he seemed to lose all interest in the conversation and sat upright again.

"I can only assume that Maharaj wanted to corroborate his own intuitive knowledge of my past lives and that he therefore put me into this unusual state of consciousness in which I was able to tell him what he wanted to know."

VI

MYSTIC VISIONS

MAHARAJ once told me: "There are times when it becomes impossible for me to teach anyone. No matter where I look, I see only God, wearing many masks. Who am I, the teacher? Who is to be taught? How can God teach God? But when my mind comes down again, to a lower level, I see the ignorance in man and I try to remove it."

Maharaj spent most of his later life in a state of high spiritual consciousness, coming down only in order to teach and help us. His awareness of God had become so habitual that he would experience mystical visions even while conscious of the external world around him. He rarely spoke of these visions, and when he did so it was only to his brother-swamis or disciples.

Vijnanananda, a disciple of Sri Ramakrishna, said of Maharaj and his visions: "The gods and goddesses are not myths, they are real. They are the many aspects of the one Godhead. I know this because Maharaj used to see and talk to them." I shall record a few of Maharaj's visions in this chapter.

It was the year 1901, a few days before the annual worship of Durga—God the Mother in her aspect as protectress of the universe. Maharaj was sitting on the bank of the Ganges at the Belur Math. Suddenly he saw Mother Durga walking on the surface of the Ganges toward the monastery grounds. She passed under the sacred vilwa tree in the monastery garden and then disappeared. A moment later Swamiji arrived by boat, came to Maharaj, and said: "Raja, make arrangements at once for the worship of Mother Durga." Then he told Maharaj that he had had a vision, and had seen Mother Durga being worshiped at the monastery. Maharaj, in turn, described his own vision to Swamiji, and they began at once to prepare for the worship. Since that date the special worship of Mother Durga has been held every year at the Belur Monastery. Maharaj also performed this worship at the monasteries in Kankhal, Benares, and Madras. He once told Akhilananda that he performed this worship in obedience to the Mother's direct command. Akhilananda records that, during the Durga festival in Madras, the power of Maharaj was specially felt by his disciples, and their minds were raised to higher levels of spirituality.

Maharaj used to observe Christmas every year by offering special worship to Jesus. The story of the Nativity was read aloud from the Bible and followed by meditation. Fruit, bread, cake, and wine were offered in the worship.

Sister Devamata, an American devotee who happened to be present on one such occasion records the scene as follows:

"When I had finished reading, the intense stillness in the air led me to look towards Swami Brahmananda. His eyes were open and fixed on the altar, there was a smile on his lips, but it was evident that his consciousness had gone to a higher plane. No one moved or spoke. At the end of twenty minutes or more, the look of immediate seeing returned to his eyes and he motioned to us to continue the service."

After the service, as Maharaj was partaking of the sacramental food, he remarked to Sister Devamata: "While you were reading, Christ suddenly stood before the altar, dressed in a long blue cloak. He talked to me for some time. It was a very blessed moment."

Swami Vishwananda relates the following incident: "One day Ram Nam was sung in Maharaj's small room at the Udbodhan office, where he was staying while Holy Mother was visiting her native village. There were only half a dozen people present. Maharaj was repeatedly in ecstasy. Sometimes his body shook, sometimes it was stiff. He uttered a few syllables expressing great joy. The place became surcharged with spiritual vibrations. I felt I was transported to another realm. When the singing was over, an attendant of Swami Premananda saluted

Maharaj before taking his leave. As he bowed down to him, Maharaj exclaimed: 'Foolish boy, where will you go now? What happened here was more than meditation!' The implication was clear. Why should the brahmachari leave this spot where God-consciousness was so tangible?

"In Maharaj's presence we understood the meaning of these words: 'The guru expounds the texts of the scriptures in silence. The doubts of the disciples are dispelled.' "

The guru sees directly into the inner nature of the spiritual seeker and addresses himself to the aspirant's highest yearnings. On an afternoon of a beautiful spring day in March 1916, a young Indian girl came to the monastery to see Maharaj. Forced into marriage by her parents, she had run away from her husband to the monastery, and as soon as she was brought into the presence of Maharaj, she fell at his feet saying: "O father, I have no desire to live a worldly life. I wish only to spend my days here at the monastery under your guidance. My one desire is to worship God and realize him. To him alone I would surrender myself, body, mind, and soul." Deeply touched by her evident earnestness and guilelessness of character, Maharaj replied: "My child, this is a monastery! How can you stay here? Go back to your parents; they are worried about you. Stay with them; study the scriptures and read the teachings of Sri Ramakrishna and Swami Vivekananda. Pray to Sri Ramakrishna. He knows the yearnings of your heart and will answer your prayers. Later on you may go to the Nivedita school for girls, or to the ashrama of Gouri-Ma. You have the true understanding. Vain indeed is this human birth unless one has love for God!" But the young girl refused to return to her parents' home, so Maharaj blessed her and sent her to the ashrama.

After she had left, Maharaj walked slowly into the library where he found Swami Premananda writing a letter. He sat down beside him, and almost immediately went into a mood of ecstasy. Those who watched him could catch only a glimpse of the ecstatic joy which shone through his radiant face. His expression and behavior were indescribable. Swami Premananda watched him for a while, then, turning to the young monk who was also present, said: "Watch Maharaj! That mood in which you see him is known as the *paramahamsa* state!"

In a little while, Maharaj returned to normal consciousness, and said to Swami Premananda: "Who can understand the divine play of Sri Ramakrishna? Swami Vivekananda wanted to see a convent established for young women, and now I see that some day soon his desire will be fulfilled. Young women are becoming imbued with the ideal of renunciation as taught by our master. That girl who came today was like a goddess in her beauty, her purity, her earnestness, and her guilelessness!"

THERE IS A SAYING in Sanskrit: "Places of pilgrimage are made holy by the visits of the seers of God." The enlightened soul does not need to visit holy places or temples, for he has realized the living God everywhere. Wherever he lives, that place becomes holy. Nevertheless, we know that enlightened men often journey to shrines and temples. They do so because they find there a greater manifestation of God—a more concentrated revelation, as it were.

This spiritual concentration has been caused by the visits of many holy men and women and by the devotion of pilgrims throughout the ages. When a saint goes to a holy place, he contributes his own revelation to the spiritual treasure house for the benefit of the generations that will follow.

The temples of India are dedicated to deities of many forms and aspects as well as to the impersonal, formless Godhead. This one Godhead, whose name is Silence, comprises all divine forms and aspects, yet is beyond form and definition. Sri Ramakrishna used to say: "Never set a limit to the Infinite by trying to define it." And indeed, it is evident that the infinite God must have infinite forms of expression. "Truth is one, sages call it by various names," says the Rig-Veda, the ancient scripture of the Hindus.

In an orchestra, different instruments play different notes, but when these notes are harmonized the combined effect is of one beautiful unity. Maharaj reached this unity through his realization of Brahman. An ordinary mystic may be aware of only one instrument and hear only one note—one part or aspect of the divine whole. The illumined soul, however, hears all the instruments, the entire orchestra.

Thus it was that Maharaj, while ever conscious of the one Brahman, was able to see the many divine aspects when he visited the temples dedicated to them.

At Madura, in Southern India, there is a famous temple of Divine Mother. When Maharaj entered it and stood before the deity, he exclaimed: "Mother, Mother!" and lost his external consciousness. Swami Ramakrishnananda, who was with him, saw his condition and held him by the arms to prevent him from falling. Seeing Maharaj standing unconscious in ecstasy, the priests and devotees who were present gazed at him in silence. An intense stillness pervaded the temple and lasted for more than an hour. When Maharaj regained his normal consciousness he went silently away. Later he described his vision of the luminous form of Divine Mother. At the temple of Rameswar, which is dedicated to Shiva, the formless aspect of God, Maharaj was again absorbed in samadhi. Even after he returned to normal consciousness, he remained for some time in a state of ecstatic joy.

The temple at Cape Comorin is dedicated to Divine Mother in the form of a little girl. Maharaj lived there for several days. For a while he would stand silent and motionless before the deity; then he would become ecstatic and begin to talk to her. Whenever he entered this temple, he lost all external consciousness. In the temple of Vishnu at Tirupati in Southern India, Maharaj had a strange experience. The vision he beheld there was not of Vishnu, but of Divine

Mother. On inquiry it was found that the temple had once been dedicated to Mother, and later had been changed into a Vishnu temple through the influence of Ramanuja.

In the temple of Jagannath at Puri, there are three images. Sri Krishna stands on one side, his brother, Balaram, on the other, and Subhadra, his sister, stands in the center. Here Maharaj once saw the living Krishna on the altar; the three images had disappeared. Maharaj visited this temple many times, and each time he went there he seemed to dwell in another realm, and his face shone with a radiant smile.

Of the many places of pilgrimage that Maharaj visited, he loved Brindaban and Benares most of all. He used to tell us that in these two cities a spiritual current is always flowing, and that this current grows particularly strong at certain times of the day and night. He said that if a man meditates and practices japam in Brindaban at midnight he is greatly helped by the spiritual current, and if he meditates in Benares at four o'clock in the morning he may easily become absorbed into the higher consciousness. In later years when Maharaj visited the temples at Brindaban and Benares, he would ask his disciples to sing and chant and he himself would go into samadhi.

Speaking of Benares, he said: "Many have found enlightenment there. If the aspirant struggles a little to reach union with God, he may get it very easily." Only once did Maharaj initiate a disciple in Benares.

After that he refused to do so, because, as he said: "Lord Shiva gives liberation to all those who live and die there." A disciple, who later became Swami Akhilananda, was once in Benares with Maharaj and wanted initiation. "Holy Mother does not initiate any disciple in Benares," Maharaj told him. "I have made the same rule." Then in a sweet affectionate voice he added: "I will initiate you when I go back to the monastery at Belur. Don't be impatient. In my mind I have already accepted you as my disciple and have made myself responsible for you."

Once, during the celebration of Sri Ramakrishna's birthday at Belur, while the disciples were singing and chanting, Maharaj went into samadhi. He was carried to his room, completely unconscious of the outer world, his face shining with a heavenly radiance. He remained in this condition so long that his brother-disciples became anxious. They told Holy Mother, who was present at the time, but she showed no anxiety; indeed she seemed well pleased, and said: "Do not worry about him." Then she went to Maharaj, touched his arm lightly and said in an affectionate voice: "Rakhal, I have brought sacramental food for you. Eat, my child." Maharaj immediately returned to normal consciousness and, seeing Holy Mother, prostrated himself at her feet.

He used to say: "It is very hard to understand Mother's greatness, unless she herself reveals it. Through the grace of Sri Ramakrishna, one may recognize the Divine Mother in her."

Once, while Maharaj was visiting Holy Mother, a female disciple of Sri Ramakrishna said to him: "Rakhal, Mother wanted to know from you why a spiritual aspirant must worship the Divine Mother first." Maharaj answered: "Mother has the key to the knowledge of Brahman. Unless she shows her grace and opens the door, no one can enter into the realm of Brahman."

As he left the house where Holy Mother was staying, Maharaj began to sing and dance, clapping his hands like a little boy. Whenever he was with Holy Mother, he always acted in this childlike manner which expressed the relationship between them.

ONCE AKHILANANDA, who was then a very young boy, was told by Swami Vijnanananda to say to Maharaj when he met him: "There is something within me that needs awakening—please give me your help." Akhilananda repeated these words to Maharaj, who replied: "Why didn't you ask Vijnanananda to do this awakening for you?" Akhilananda answered that he had, but that Swami Vijnanananda had said: "I have very little spiritual power within me, but Maharaj lives in the power-house. He can easily do what you ask." Maharaj looked very serious and said: "Yes, the awakening will come. Don't be impatient. For this awakening one needs initiation."

"Then please initiate me."

"That will be done," Maharaj promised.

To quote Akhilananda's own words: "Maharaj made us feel that spiritual awakening and God-realization are not difficult to achieve. He made us understand that if only we will struggle a little, tremendous help will be given us, and that we shall easily reach the goal."

In his later years Maharaj had the vision of Sri Ramakrishna every day. He used to tell me: "I see Sri Ramakrishna every day and talk to him." To another disciple he said: "I see Sri Ramakrishna whenever he chooses to reveal himself to me. By his grace, you also will see him and talk to him."

Although Maharaj lived almost continuously in a high state of consciousness, he was very natural and human in his behavior. Even when he was quite a young man, Sri Ramakrishna said of him: "Rakhal is like the kind of mango which still looks green outside when it is ripe and sweet within." And this was true throughout his life. Whenever he could, he would hide his ecstatic mood and act in the most normal way. I have already mentioned his sense of humor. Balaram's wife once dreamt that she was feeding Maharaj. Taking this for an omen, she invited him to a sumptuous feast which she herself cooked. When Maharaj had enjoyed the dinner, he turned to her grandson and said: "Tell your grandmother to dream more often."

His love of gardening has been referred to in an earlier chapter. At every monastery he visited, he gave valuable advice as to the laying out of gardens.

Often he would gaze at the blossoming flowers and remark: "Look! There you see the worship of God in his universal form going on unceasingly."

Maharaj also loved music. He always had a band of musicians or a singer with him. Maharaj himself did not sing much—just occasionally a line or so. But every morning he would chant the various names of the Lord in his sweet voice. One day a fine musician was playing musical scales. Maharaj went into a spiritual mood. A devotee complained that no devotional songs were being played. This jarred Maharaj. He turned to the devotee and said: "Don't you realize that sound is Brahman?"

One day at the Ramakrishna Math in Madras I was in the monastery's library, whose door opens onto a large hallway. The shrine is directly above. As I opened the library door, I suddenly saw Maharaj in the distance, with arms outstretched, moving about the hall as though he were dancing. He was alone and completely absorbed in God. Speechless with amazement, I watched him, thrilled by the sight. Suddenly his eyes fell upon me, and with arms still outstretched he advanced in my direction. However, I at once began to feel nervous and started to back away. I did not consider myself pure enough to touch Maharaj while he was in such a lofty mood, and I was afraid that my presence might disturb his ecstasy. So I silently shut the library door and went away.

MANY OF HIS householder disciples came to Maharaj with their worldly troubles and problems. Not only did he listen to them sympathetically, but he also gave them constructive advice. Many successful professional men, such as doctors, lawyers, engineers, found it very easy to discuss the problems of their work with Maharaj. He would listen with intelligent interest and understanding, and was often able to offer a new suggestion or another angle of approach to the problem.

Even though he was interested in everything and in all the events of his time, his intimate disciples could see that beneath this apparent interest Maharaj always remained completely detached. The things of this world rolled off him like drops of water off a lotus leaf.

VII

HIS PASSING

I HAVE already described how Sri Ramakrishna saw
Rakhal dancing with Sri Krishna on a mystic lotus
shortly before the boy's first visit to Dakshineswar.
Only a few intimate disciples knew of this vision, and
Sri Ramakrishna had warned them never to reveal it
to Maharaj, explaining that if he realized his true
nature as the Eternal Companion of Krishna, he
would leave his mortal body. The secret had therefore been very carefully guarded.

In March 1922, Maharaj went to Calcutta to stay
for a while at the home of Balaram. Balaram himself
had already passed away, but his whole family were
sincere devotees of Ramakrishna, and his beautiful
guesthouse was always at the disposal of all the swamis and disciples of the Order.

It is now regarded as a place of pilgrimage, sanctified by the presence of so many holy men.

While Maharaj was staying at the guesthouse,
Ramlal Dada came to visit him. Ramlal Dada was a

pure soul and a devotee of a very high order. During
Ramakrishna's lifetime, he had been one of the Master's personal attendants and had served him with
great devotion. Whenever he and Maharaj were together, their talk naturally turned to the early days.
They would laugh and joke together, for they stimu-
lated each other's sense of fun. One day Maharaj
asked Ramlal Dada to sing for him the songs he used
to sing to Ramakrishna. It was arranged that many
disciples and devotees should be present to hear the
singing.

Ramlal Dada began to sing songs about Krishna
and the shepherds and shepherdesses of Brindaban.
At first, everyone was very gay as Ramlal mimicked
the gestures of the shepherdesses, making his audience laugh. Suddenly, Maharaj, who had also been
enjoying the fun, became serious. Ramlal Dada was
singing: "Come back, O Krishna, come back to Brindaban. Come and reign in the hearts of your beloved
shepherds and shepherdesses. Do not forget that you
are a shepherd yourself." At that moment Maharaj
seemed transported to a realm beyond this earth. The
joking and laughter stopped. The atmosphere became
calm and serene. It may be that at this moment
Maharaj got a partial glimpse of his true nature and
knew himself to be God's Eternal Companion. The
events that followed seem to point to some such revelation.

A few days later, at midnight, Nirvanananda, a
disciple and personal attendant of Maharaj, saw his

master sitting on his bed in a very earnest mood. The disciple stood silently before him, waiting for him to speak. Maharaj looked at him, and said: "I woke suddenly and saw Sri Ramakrishna standing just there." He pointed to a spot in front of a couch, adding: "He didn't speak to me. He stood there silently for a while and then disappeared. I don't understand it."

After a few moments Maharaj continued in a low, earnest voice: "I can't give my mind to the things of this world any longer. It wants to take complete refuge in him and him alone."

Shortly after this, the birthday of Sri Ramakrishna was celebrated. Maharaj stayed at the Belur Math for the occasion; then he returned to Balaram's house in Calcutta. Two days later he had a slight attack of cholera, but recovered within a week. This illness which left him feeble was followed by diabetes, which took a serious turn. Many doctors came to treat him, one of whom wore the religious mark on his forehead.

"Doctor," said Maharaj, "the Lord Shiva, whose symbol you wear on your forehead, is the only Reality. Everything else is unreal."

A devotee asked: "Maharaj, are you suffering very greatly?"

"Please try to realize," Maharaj answered, "that in my condition I have to bear all physical suffering patiently and without complaint."

But as he said this, his face lighted up with a divine radiance. The pain seemed to have melted away. He lost external consciousness and became absorbed in meditation.

About nine o'clock that same evening, he placed his hand on Nirvanananda, and said: "Do not grieve. You have served me well. You shall be merged in God and reach knowledge of Brahman. I give you my blessing that you may attain this."

Then he called all the disciples and devotees who were present to his side. For each he had a blessing and an affectionate word.

"Ah, my children," he said tenderly, "never forget God and you will realize the highest good. Do not sorrow. I shall be with you always."

Once more he became absorbed in his transcendental vision. After some time had passed, he continued in a sweet, tender voice: "I am floating, I am floating on the leaf of faith and knowledge on the ocean of Brahman." Then suddenly he exclaimed: "Ah! The feet of Sri Ramakrishna—I know them! Viveka, my brother Vivekananda! Premananda . . . Yogananda . . ."

Thus, with his divine sight, he recognized the brother-disciples who had already passed away. He was living in that transcendental realm where he had lived throughout his life; but now he no longer concealed the fact. He began to describe his visions.

"Ah," he murmured softly, "the blissful ocean of Brahman! Om! Salutations to the Supreme Brahman! Om! Salutations to the Supreme Atman!"

While speaking of his divine experiences, his throat

became dry. A disciple offered him a drink, saying: "Maharaj, please drink this water. It has lemon in it."

"The mind doesn't want to come down from Brahman," said Maharaj slowly. "Pour Brahman into Brahman," and like a child he opened his mouth for the water to be poured into it.

Then he turned to Swami Saradananda and said: "Brother, Sri Ramakrishna is real. His divine incarnation is real."

After this Maharaj was silent for a while. He was deeply absorbed in meditation, and his face wore an expression of great sweetness. The minds of those who were present were so uplifted that they felt no grief—only joy and silent calm. All sense of the world and of death was lost.

Suddenly, out of the silence, the voice of Maharaj was heard: "Ah, that inexpressible light! Ramakrishna, the Krishna of my Ramakrishna . . . I am the shepherd boy. Put anklets on my feet, I want to dance with my Krishna. I want to hold his hand—the little boy Krishna . . . Ah, Krishna, my Krishna, you have come! Krishna . . . Krishna . . . Can't you see him? Haven't you eyes to see? Oh, how beautiful! My Krishna . . . on the lotus . . . eternal . . . the Sweet One!

"My play is over now. Look! The child Krishna is caressing me. He is calling me to come away with him! I am coming . . ."

The tenderness and heavenly compassion that

filled his heart were expressed in every word he uttered.

The whole atmosphere of the large hall where he was lying seemed to vibrate with this emotion. No one can describe the extraordinary sense of holiness which was created by his presence. Everyone knew that the fateful hour was approaching, and that Maharaj was taking his final leave.

During the early hours of the morning, he remained silent for some time and fell into a slumber. At seven o'clock he awoke, and was again possessed by this high spiritual mood. He called the few disciples who had just arrived but who had not been present the previous night. To each he gave his blessing, bestowing comfort and fearlessness.

Two more days passed, and another night came on. By this time his life was despaired of, and gloom fell upon all. His physical condition grew worse and worse, and the doctors were amazed that he had not passed into a coma days before, as is usual with this kind of illness. But so great was the power and spirituality of his mind, so completely was it freed from the meshes of physical matter, that it remained completely unaffected by the condition of his suffering body. He maintained perfect consciousness right up to the last moment of his life.

As that last evening faded into night, his chest suddenly heaved. It was as if a great wave of breath passed up the body to the throat. His half-closed eyes opened, and he gazed into the distance, his eyes shining with a brilliance and unspeakable beauty.

Thus it was that, on April 10, 1922, the life left his body.

"Do not grieve. I shall be with you always." Those were his last words to his disciples. After his passing away, we all had the feeling that Maharaj was intensely present within us. He was closer to us than ever before. As long as Maharaj was in the physical body there was a barrier. Afterward, the barrier was gone.

More than forty years have passed since that day, and every disciple can bear witness to the fact that Maharaj still lives, protects, and guides him onward toward the goal.

When I was about to leave India and take up my duties in the United States, Swami Shivananda said to me: "Never forget that you have seen the Son of God. You have seen God."

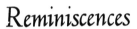

Reminiscences

SWAMI AMBIKANANDA

MY PARENTS WERE DEVOTEES OF Sri Ramakrishna and often visited him at Dakshineswar. During her pregnancy my mother decided that if a son was born to her she would dedicate him to the service of Sri Ramakrishna. Through the grace of the Lord I was the son born to her. She resolved to keep her promise. One day, when I was a few weeks old, my mother carried me snugly bundled up in a sheet to Dakshineswar. My father accompanied us. Sri Ramakrishna, in an ecstatic mood, was standing alone. As soon as he saw my parents, he said to my mother: "Hello, what have you brought for me?" Mother placed me at the feet of the Master and replied: "I have brought you this offering." Sri Ramakrishna looked at me for a few moments and remarked: "Ah! What a nice child! Are you offering it to me? Good!" He took me on his lap, put his right palm on my head as a blessing, and then placed me back in my mother's arms, saying: "Take care of this child now, but know that he belongs to me. In due time I will take him back." Years later, when I joined the Ramakrishna Monastery, my mother was the happiest of all, for she felt that Sri Ramakrishna had accepted me. (Sri Ramakrishna had then passed away.)

As a young boy I used to visit the monastery at Alambazar with my parents. The Belur Math was not yet founded. Swamis Brahmananda, Ramakrishnananda, Shivananda, Turiyananda, and Advaitananda were living there at the time. Sometimes I would stay at the monastery for several days. I thought of Maharaj as being very stern, and would carefully avoid him. Swami Turiyananda was affectionate toward me, and I felt free with him. The nights I passed in the monastery I used to sleep in the same room with Swami Turiyananda. He used to wake up at midnight and would wake me also at that hour to meditate.

After Swami Vivekananda passed away, Maharaj and Swami Turiyananda went to Brindaban and practiced austerities. A short time thereafter, my father and I went there also. Whenever my father visited the swamis I would accompany him. As I knew Swami Turiyananda intimately, I would pass most of my time in his company. Maharaj lived in a room adjoining his. Every time I called on Swami Turiyananda, I would prostrate before him, then slowly open the door to Maharaj's room and bow down to Maharaj from the door. I was nervous in his presence, regarding him as very serious and austere, and so would not go inside the room to prostrate or touch his feet. Watching my behavior one day, Swami Turiyananda remarked: "What is this? Go in, prostrate before Maharaj, and touch his blessed feet." With trepidation in my heart I entered the room, did as I was told, and then stood silently by Maharaj. He looked at me graciously and said in an affectionate tone: "Child, massage my feet." With these words he lay down. I began to massage him, though still nervous. He sensed it immediately and said: "Don't be nervous, my son." He touched my back, and with his touch there came a complete transformation in me. I seemed to lose all strength of body and helplessly lay down at his feet. Facetiously Maharaj said: "Ah, you are making a pillow of my feet instead of massaging them!" My heart was filled with an unspeakable joy. I sat up and said: "You have done something to me." Then I began to laugh, being unable to hold the joy within. All my fear was gone, and for the first time I had a taste of God's love emanating from Maharaj. Afterward I heard that Maharaj remarked jokingly to Swami Turiyananda: "You see, I have stolen your disciple," and that Swami Turiyananda laughed and said: "Splendid! Now the boy is blessed indeed."

At the earnest request of Swami Premananda, Maharaj left for Belur Math. Father and I accompanied him. On our way to Belur, Maharaj expressed the desire to visit the Divine Mother's temple at the Vindhyachala mountains.

The first night Maharaj, my father, our host,

Yogindra Sen, a devotee, and I slept in the same room. It was nearing midnight when I felt a gentle touch. I woke up. I saw Maharaj dressed and covered with a heavy blanket. He said to me: "Get up and dress yourself in warm clothing. I want you to come with me." Without any hesitation I did as I was told, though it did not occur to me at the time to inquire where we were going. Maharaj took a lantern in one hand and a stick in the other, and asked me to follow him. We went outside. It was the night of the new moon and pitch-dark. The path was uneven. Realizing that I was stumbling, Maharaj gave me the lantern to carry and held me by the hand. I asked him then: "Where are we going?" He replied: "To see the Divine Mother."

When we entered the temple compound we found the place crowded with worshipers. Some were counting beads and others were chanting the praises of the Divine Mother. There was an intense spiritual atmosphere. The door of the temple was still closed. The priests were decorating Mother's image for the special occasion. When the doors opened, the pilgrims stood up and moved forward slowly to have the *darshan* of Mother. In the meantime the priests caught sight of Maharaj. Seeing his benign face and impressed by his personality, they stopped the pilgrims from proceeding and let Maharaj enter first. He was still holding my hand, and I was following him. When Maharaj stood before the image of Divine Mother, he exclaimed: "Ah! How beautiful, how beautiful!'' The next moment he was in ecstasy. There was perfect silence in the temple. The priests and pilgrims watched Maharaj's God-intoxicated state in amazement. After a while, still in an ecstatic mood, Maharaj asked me to sing a song to Divine Mother. While I was singing, tears of joy fell from the outer corners of his eyes. It was a divine sight to behold. Maharaj asked me to sing another song, after which we prostrated before the Mother and came out into the courtyard. Maharaj sat down in one corner to perform japam and asked me to sit also. I said: "What shall I do?" Maharaj replied: "Think of the presence of Divine Mother. Later I shall instruct you." We stayed for a while and returned to Yogindra Sen's before daybreak.

At the foot of a mountain near Vindhyachala there is a cave temple. One day we went with some other devotees to a picnic nearby. While the devotees were busy preparing vegetables and getting ready to cook, Maharaj asked me to follow him. We began to climb the mountain and reached the door of the cave temple. It was pitch-dark inside. We entered the cave and proceeded slowly until we came near the deity. It was very quiet, not even the noise of a bird could be heard. Maharaj sat by the image of Divine Mother, and I sat near him. After some time he asked me to sing the praises of Mother. While listening to the song, Maharaj went into ecstasy, as he had done in the other temple. First his body shook a little, the hair of the body stood on end, and tears of joy ran down his cheeks. Then he became perfectly still. He was completely unconscious. I was not worried, because I had heard of Sri Ramakrishna going into samadhi in this way.

After some time Maharaj slowly regained his normal consciousness, and we came out of the cave. I thought that we would now return to the picnic grounds, but instead Maharaj began to climb higher up the mountain. I followed him. We reached the summit. Maharaj seated himself on a rock in yoga posture and asked me to do the same. While sitting, I thought to myself: "Well, Maharaj has asked me to sit here, but he has not yet instructed me." I asked him on what and how I should meditate. His answer was: "Meditate on any aspect of God that appeals to you."

Another day we climbed the mountain from a different side. When we reached the summit, the sun was setting. Maharaj asked me to sing the following song:

> The day is gone, O my mind,
> What preparations have you made
> To cross this ocean of worldliness?
> The sun of life is about to set.
> Though you see it setting, you pay no heed.
> Deluded by the maya of this ephemeral world,
>   you lose the treasure eternal.

While listening, Maharaj became absorbed in meditation. After the song he remained in that state for a while. It was getting dark, and we went home.

Thus, instead of the three days that Maharaj had originally intended to stay at Vindhyachala, we spent twenty-one days there before Maharaj returned to Belur Math.

SWAMI NIRVANANANDA

I MET MAHARAJ for the first time in the Ramakrishna Mission Sevashrama of Benares, which is a hospital for the suffering and destitute. The monks and novices of the ashrama serve the patients with devotion as manifestations of God. Inspired by this noble ideal of the Ramakrishna Order, I joined the ashrama with an ardent desire to become a monk. I had corresponded with Maharaj before our first meeting, and I had read about him in the *Gospel of Sri Ramakrishna.*

In the midst of the busy program of the Sevashrama, the thought would linger in my mind: "When shall I go and see Maharaj?" His eyes always revealed his sympathy and otherworldliness. And his radiant, smiling face and the sweetness of his childlike simplicity attracted me to him more and more.

At the end of my daily routine, whenever the opportunity presented itself, I never failed to be near Maharaj and to wait on him, just to be permitted to do some personal service. Through such service, sometimes I felt flashes of joy within myself. I was firmly convinced that it was essential for me to have the company of this blessed soul, without whose light

I felt there was no way for me to understand or conceive Brahman, Atman, God, and other entities that exist beyond sense-perception.

According to Sri Ramakrishna's direction, Swami Vivekananda had delivered the charge of the Order to Maharaj who, on Swamiji's passing away, set himself heart and soul to the great responsibility given to him. Through his uncommon personality and spiritual power the Order progressed day by day. From Maharaj's countenance, no one could guess his leadership and potentiality. He was totally free from any attachment to the fruits of work, such as hope, signs of dejection, pride of prestige, or efforts to exhibit power.

Whether in the forest or in the city, Maharaj led a very simple life. Wherever he stayed, monks and devotees flocked around him. Those who came to see him went back overwhelmed by his piety and his pure and unselfish love toward all. By a glance or a touch or his mere presence, he could raise the minds of others to a high level and change their very lives. This will be apparent from some of the incidents in his life which we will mention here.

A PROFESSOR from Calcutta University had read about Maharaj in the *Gospel of Sri Ramakrishna.* Having learned what a great soul he was, he decided to visit him. I happened to be serving as Maharaj's personal attendant at Balaram Bose's house where he was staying at the time. Balaram's son, who was a great devotee, had a room especially furnished for Maharaj and had presented him with a beautiful silk robe. One day, while I was away, the professor entered Maharaj's room unannounced. Seeing Maharaj smoking a hookah, surrounded by luxury, was a tremendous shock to him. This was Ramakrishna's spiritual son, whom he had imagined as so austere! Without introducing himself to Maharaj, he left the room. But he did not go away; he sat outside on the veranda and thought about the experience he had just had. When I returned, I saw the professor seated on a bench on the veranda. Unaware that the visitor had already been to Maharaj's room, I approached him and asked, "Would you like to see Maharaj?" The professor thought for a moment and said, "Yes, I would." So he was ushered in, and Maharaj welcomed him. When the professor came out of Maharaj's room about an hour later, he told me: "I almost made the greatest mistake of my life. I was going to judge Maharaj by externals, with my own idea of spirituality. . . . Now the deepest problem of my life has been solved." Later he became a disciple of Maharaj.

DEVENDRANATH BOSE (called Deven Babu—*Babu* means "Mister") was a devotee of Sri Ramakrishna and friendly with all his direct disciples, particularly with Swami Akhandananda. After the passing away of the Master, Deven Babu became the estate manager of the maharaja of Kashim Bazar, and for many years he did not come to see the monks.

One day, Swami Akhandananda met Deven Babu by chance and brought him to the Belur Math. Maharaj was at the monastery at the time. On seeing Deven Babu after such a long interval, Maharaj said to Swami Akhandananda: "Well, Gangadhar, what has happened to your Deven? He has changed very much—in movements, manners, everything. His face has a worldly expression, and he dresses like a dandy. Has he forgotten the Master and all of us?"

Swami Akhandananda did not know what to say. But the next time he saw Deven Babu, he told him in the course of conversation what Maharaj had said about him.

"I don't know what has happened to me. I am not happy," said Deven Babu.

After a few days, Deven Babu came to see Maharaj. I was sitting in front of Maharaj's room. Deven Babu asked me: "Where is Maharaj?"

I said to him: "Please take a seat. Maharaj is in his room. I shall inform him of your arrival."

Deven Babu's great restlessness was clearly visible. He was unable to sit still. Seeing Deven Babu, Maharaj silently went to him. He placed his hand on Deven Babu's chest, stroked it several times, and said: "Everything will be all right. Think of the Master!"

Immediately there was a complete change in Deven Babu. He bowed down before Maharaj and said: "Maharaj, all my worldliness is wiped out. How far I had fallen! But your grace and blessings have lifted me up. Now I have no more sorrows or troubles."

Long after the passing away of Maharaj Deven Babu wrote about him: "Those who came in close contact with the spiritual son of the Master say that Maharaj was endowed with immeasurable spiritual splendor. . . . But nobody knew how so much power could be contained within that mortal frame.

"The latent power of an electric wire is known only on touching it. We hear that the body of a realized soul is not made of matter but of spirit. But that truth could not be understood even while coming in touch with this divine man. With what heavenly love Maharaj kept us deluded!"

Deven Babu once said to me: "Do you remember the occasion when I went to see Maharaj? When he touched my chest with his hand, I felt a sudden shock. Immediately I remembered my past; love for God and yearning for realization filled me, and all the memories of the Master came alive again in my mind. As a result, the course of my life was altogether changed."

THE FOLLOWING INCIDENT illustrates how Maharaj disciplined those in his charge.

Three young brahmacharis were at one time connected with the revolutionary movement. After joining the monastery they were still under the surveillance of the police. Every third day, the police would come to the Math to check that they were there.

On one occasion these boys went to a place of pilgrimage and did not return to the Math on time, which caused much embarrassment to Maharaj. When they finally arrived, Maharaj took them to task and then expelled them from the monastery. As the brahmacharis were leaving, they met Swami Premananda at the gate. They told him the whole story. Swami Premananda advised them not to leave the compound, but to hide under a tree and to pray. This they did.

While Maharaj was having lunch he asked me to order some delicacies from Calcutta, which I received within a couple of hours. After Maharaj got up from his noonday rest, he inquired whether the special food he had asked for had arrived. I had no idea what it was all about, but I answered: "Yes, Maharaj, I have everything ready."

Then he asked: "Do you know where those three brahmacharis are?"

I replied: "No, Maharaj, I haven't seen them."

Maharaj said: "Go and find them!"

I went into the garden, and in a short time I found the three boys under a tree and asked them to go and see Maharaj. When they came to his room, Maharaj told them to forget all about the episode. Then he added: "We are holy men, and our anger is just like a mark on water. . . . Now eat this food!"

AFTER MANY YEARS Maharaj was asked to look at a statue someone had made of Sri Ramakrishna to see whether it was a good likeness. Maharaj asked: "In what form has the sculptor made it?" The meaning of his question becomes clear if we keep in mind that the Master appeared to him in many aspects of divinity.

Maharaj laid much stress on the significance of the Master's advent. When such an Incarnation comes to earth much power is manifested, and with little effort a spiritual aspirant becomes illumined.

One day Maharaj said to M., the recorder of *The Gospel of Sri Ramakrishna:* "The Master came this time to make a bridge between *jiva* and Shiva (man and God). See how easy it has now become to realize the Lord!"

Maharaj used to tell us: "Don't waste this opportunity! Be up and doing! Once you lose this chance you will regret it. Sri Ramakrishna was the epitome of truth. Mold your lives according to this ideal. Those of you who are working in the hospital will also be able to reach the goal and realize the Reality through the practice of pure, unselfish work."

SRI RAMAKRISHNA used to say: "Rakhal is my son— my spiritual son." The fact that this relationship remained intact even after the Master's passing away may be understood from the following incident.

It was in the year 1918. Maharaj was then staying at Balaram Bose's house in the Baghbazar section of Calcutta. I was with him, being his attendant at the time. On this particular day Maharaj had just finished his lunch. Generally he took a rest about this time.

I was sitting on a bench outside his room when a young girl and her brother arrived. The girl asked permission to see Maharaj. I told her that it would not be convenient for him to see her now.

She began to cry. Swami Saradananda had told her to come, and pleadingly she asked: "Look, I shall only prostrate before him and then go. Please arrange it for me!"

Moved by her plight, I again went to Maharaj. I told him: "Sarat Maharaj has sent this girl. She only wants to bow down and then she will go." After I mentioned Swami Saradananda's name Maharaj agreed to see her.

Later I learned that while prostrating, the girl began to sob, overwhelmed with emotion. Maharaj suddenly went into an ecstatic mood and became silent and motionless. After a while he looked at the girl and said: "Get up, my child; tell me what has happened." But the girl was still weeping. She stood up but was not able to speak for some time. Then, pointing to a picture of Sri Ramakrishna which Maharaj had in his room, she said: "He has asked me to come to you."

She told her story. She was married at the age of fourteen. Only two weeks after their marriage her husband died. (In India this was a disastrous situation because at that time a Hindu widow could not remarry nor work to support herself, and had to depend mostly on her parents or other near relatives to care for her.) Her future looked very dark, and in her

despair she wept bitterly and incessantly prayed to
God: "O Lord, what will become of me? I am so
lonely and helpless. What shall I do? Please show me
the way!" After a year or so, one night Sri Ramakrishna appeared to her in a dream and said: "Don't
weep. My son Rakhal is living in Baghbazar. Go to
him. He will help you." She did not know anything
about Sri Ramakrishna or Rakhal, and she wondered
how she could get to Baghbazar which was in another
section of Calcutta, far from where she lived. She did
not mention her dream to anybody in her father-in-
law's household, went to her mother, and told her
everything. Her mother knew about Sri Ramakrishna. On learning about him from her, the girl
went to Baghbazar with her brother. There she inquired if a holy man lived nearby. She was told that
several holy men were living at the Udbodhan publi-
cation house of the Ramakrishna Order. Swami
Saradananda was staying there at the time. She told
him about her vision of Sri Ramakrishna, and the
Swami sent her to Balaram Mandir to see Maharaj.

The girl was with Maharaj for more than two
hours. Finally he called me. As I entered the room,
I noticed that the girl had received initiation. Maharaj asked me to get some food for her and her brother.
After this meeting, the girl came often to see Maharaj. And I saw her once or twice at the monastery
after Maharaj's passing away in 1922.

In 1942, a nun in ocher-colored robes came to see
me at Belur Math. She was accompanied by a young

girl disciple. I did not recognize the nun at first; but when she reminded me of her visit with Maharaj at Balaram Mandir twenty-four years before, I at once recalled the incident and asked her where she had been all these years. She answered that, following Maharaj's instructions, she had spent her time in spiritual practices in such places of pilgrimage as Benares, Brindaban, and Hardwar. Now she was living in Calcutta near Kalighat with a few disciples. Her appearance showed a definite spiritual attainment.

About three years later, the same girl disciple who had accompanied the nun to the Belur Math came to see me. When I inquired about her teacher I was told that she had passed away two years before. During her last days she was ill. One morning she asked for an almanac to find the nearest auspicious day. On that day she asked her disciples to devote their time to prayer and meditation. She herself repeated the names of Sri Ramakrishna, Holy Mother, and Maharaj. While doing so, in full consciousness, she left the body.

SWAMI APARNANANDA

A WEEK OR SO AFTER my first visit to Swami Brahmananda, I went to the Belur Math about four o'clock in the afternoon. Ever since I met him I had been longing to see him again.

As soon as I arrived at the monastery I went to the shrineroom. When Swami Premananda saw me come

out he said: "Have you seen Maharaj? Go and see
him! He is the spiritual son of Sri Ramakrishna and
his living embodiment. When you receive the grace
and blessings of Maharaj, know that these come directly from the Master. Have firm faith in this." With
folded hands Swami Premananda bowed down, saying: "Hail Maharaj, hail Maharaj!"

With Swami Premananda's permission, the other
devotees and I went upstairs into the monastery.
Now many devotees began to gather around Maharaj, including Pulin Mitra, a well-known musician
and a disciple of Swami Vivekananda. Maharaj said:
"Pulin, I have not heard you sing for a long time. Sing
something!" Pulin sang: "Mother, in dense darkness
Thy beautiful form flashes; therefore the yogis meditate on Thee in the mountain cave . . ." Then he sang:
"There the sun shines not, nor the lightning, nor the
beautiful moon . . ." Another song followed: "The
abode of bliss, wondrously beautiful, lights the shore
beyond the ocean of worldliness . . ."

While listening to the songs Maharaj became
deeply absorbed in the thought of God. The sun was
setting. Gradually, Maharaj returned to normal consciousness. An indelible impression was made on the
minds of all present by the blissful meditative figure
of Maharaj and that divine abode.

ON OUR NEXT VISIT we found Maharaj seated in an
easy chair upstairs on the veranda facing the Ganges.

His mind was indrawn, but he forced himself to talk with us occasionally.

Maharaj: "His grace and His blessings are not lacking. But how many are there who set their sail to catch His breeze of grace? How many bend their heads to receive His blessings? People's minds are busy with trivial things. Who wants the real treasure? They talk big, but they don't strive to earn anything. They want to get everything without effort. People can manage to do all kinds of worldly work, but when it comes to keeping recollectedness of God they ask: 'But where is the time to do it?'

"Sri Ramakrishna used to say: 'Gurus can be had by the thousands, but rare is a disciple.' There are plenty of people to give advice, but how many are there to listen to it? If a man has faith in the words of his guru and follows them, then all his doubts and troubles vanish. If a man has faith in the words of his guru, God will meet all his wants. Holding him by the hand, He will lead him on the right path. What worries are there if one has received His grace? From the Lord's infinite storehouse of knowledge will come a continuous supply. He in whom a longing for God has awakened, let him rise and struggle. While sitting, or lying down, or eating, let him pray piteously to His blessed feet: 'O Lord, have mercy on me! Allow me to understand your grace!'

"He is gracious. He reveals His grace to him who seeks it with a sincere heart. As we pray to Him, He gives us dispassion, longing for Him, and right understanding. Out of thousands, perchance one desires for God.

"The Master used to tell a parable about the maid servant in a rich man's house. She talks of her master's home and possessions as hers and she brings up his children as if they were her own, but in her heart of hearts she knows that none of these belong to her. In the same way, we have to live in this world and do our duties; but in our heart of hearts we must realize that nothing belongs to us, nobody belongs to us. Our only true abode is at the lotus feet of the Lord, and that is where we must go. Shunning all forms of pride and ego, we must take shelter at His feet.

"But how many wish to take refuge in the truth and in the Lord? Everybody thinks that he is infallible. Deluded by egoism, man regards himself as very important. He does not even want to believe in the existence of God. He never seriously considers how little he can understand with his intellect. Mahamaya (the Divine Mother) alone knows in how many ways she has kept man deluded.

"We (the direct disciples of Sri Ramakrishna) only know this much: never try to limit God. Infinite are his moods and aspects. He is beyond the reach of mind and intellect. And yet, if one earnestly prays to him, he becomes attainable to the pure mind.

"Nothing can be achieved without God's grace. Take refuge in him, and he will open the gate of infinite knowledge. Do your duties in the world while taking refuge in the Lord.

"First know Him. After God-realization you may live in the world and your feet will not tread the wrong path. The world's maya will not be able to bind you. Then, no matter which way you follow—whether the way of knowledge, or the way of devotion, or the way of work—you and others will benefit immensely, and your human birth will be blessed."

WE VISITED the Belur Math in the afternoon. First we went to the shrineroom. When we came downstairs we found Swami Premananda conversing with several devotees under a mango tree.

Swami Premananda: "The Master used to say: 'Once a man fed an opium pill to a peacock. Every day thereafter the peacock would return for his dose of the drug.' So the Master has given opium to these boys. Therefore they can't stay home. They take every opportunity to come here. Blessed indeed are those whom he has attracted! 'Whom the Lord chooses, by him is He attained.' Only through His grace are loosened the bondages and delusions caused by maya."

This time again we found Maharaj seated in an easy chair on the upstairs veranda. A few devotees sat on the floor in front of him.

A devotee said: "Maharaj, I cannot control my mind. Many distracting thoughts arise. What shall I do? Will I be able to practice any spiritual disciplines? How can I worship and meditate?"

Maharaj: "Pray to the Lord. Practice with

regularity. Gradually, the mind will become inclined to worship and meditate. In the beginning the mind will refuse to come under control, but force it, urge it, entreat it in order to fix it on meditation. Faith and regularity are very important; nobody can succeed in anything without them.

"You have to practice spiritual disciplines in such a way that no matter what your circumstances may be you will follow your regular routine. Once the mind tastes sweetness in the thought of God there is nothing to fear. Seek the association of the holy so that you may acquire that taste. If anybody has tasted the nectar of God's name, is it possible for him to give up chanting it? The power of his name is such that the effect is realized whether one repeats it with feeling or mechanically. The Master used to say: 'Suppose a man is walking on the bank of the Ganges. He can bathe in the river willingly, or he may accidentally fall into it, or somebody may push him in. He will have a bath in the Ganges anyway.'

"The power of the Lord's name is great indeed. Ajamil, who was dying, was thirsty, and called his son Narayan to bring him water. Thus he attained liberation at the moment of death. (Narayan is a name of God. It is a Hindu belief that if a man utters the Lord's name at the last moment, he achieves salvation.)

"Man's mind is forever restless. It remains distracted for many reasons. Association with the holy will bring it under control. Live in the society of holy people and follow their advice. If you do, you will be saved from much grief and trouble. If your mind does not become absorbed in God, it will be impossible for you to protect yourself from the many temptations of the world. By his grace, may your mind be directed toward the Reality. Unless one is strong in His strength, one cannot save oneself from the network of maya. Be strong in His strength!

"Life is flowing by like a river. The day that is done does not return. Blessed is he who uses his time fruitfully. Through many good deeds in many past lives you have been born as a human being. Make this human birth blessed by worshiping the Lord, by meditating on him. Shankara said: 'Human birth, desire for liberation, and association with the holy— only through God's grace may we obtain these three rarest advantages!' Through the Master's grace you have all these three. Struggle to attain the Lord, and make this human birth blessed! Life is impermanent. No one knows when it will end. Exert yourself to secure that treasure which will give you immortal life. While you are young you can struggle to find God. One must strive hard to realize him. There is no danger of falling if one holds fast to the pillar while whirling round it.

"Sri Ramakrishna used to say: 'When you go to a temple in order to visit the deity, you will never see it if you spend your time doling out alms to the beggars. You must push through the crowd, enter the temple, worship the deity, and then you may do whatever you please.' "

THE NEXT TIME we went to the monastery, Swami Premananda said: "Maharaj has gone to live at Balaram Mandir. While he was at the Math his radiant presence gave light to us all. Now that he is gone it seems dark. You should go to Balaram Mandir and visit him.

"Maharaj is the shepherd boy of Brindaban, a close associate of Sri Ramakrishna. He has come to earth to perform his part in the Master's divine play. As the result of much austerity in many births one receives the grace of such a great soul as Maharaj. You boys are blessed!"

After a couple of days we went to visit Maharaj at Balaram Mandir. He received us affectionately. Then he asked: "How did you know that I am staying here?"

I answered: "We went to the monastery and could not see you there. Swami Premananda said that you were at Balaram Mandir and told us to visit you here."

Maharaj smiled a little and said: "Ah, I understand, Brother Baburam throws your burden on *me!*"

Soon Ramlal Dada, Sri Ramakrishna's nephew, arrived. Maharaj seemed very happy to have Dada with him. He took him into the drawing room, offered him a seat, and sat down beside him. Gradually devotees gathered, each prostrating before Ramlal Dada and Maharaj as they arrived. Whenever someone prostrated before Maharaj first he would object: "Oh no, first bow down to Dada! He belongs to the family of our guru; and guru and God are one. In Dada's veins flows the blood of the family into which our Lord was born."

I am sure Maharaj said these words in order to inspire the devotees with greater faith in Sri Ramakrishna and his family. (During some of Ramlal Dada's visits to Maharaj we have also observed that the latter would stand with folded hands and offer Dada a seat before he himself would sit down.) Today Maharaj seemed to be in a particularly exalted mood because Ramlal Dada's presence reminded him of the old days at Dakshineswar.

Maharaj said: "Dada, please tell us something about our Master."

Ramlal Dada: "Well, brother, in those days I for one did not recognize his greatness. I used to think: 'He is our uncle. He has received the Divine Mother's special grace, and that is why many people come to him.' "

Then, pointing to Maharaj, Ramlal Dada continued: "Really, brother, it is you who truly recognized that supreme person. Inspired by his ideal of renunciation, you gave up wife, family, and everything. That is why, having touched the philosopher's stone through his grace, you have become an heir to eternal life. And now, with both hands you are distributing to others the bliss of immortality.

"Although we are his blood relatives, we did not realize who he was. But through his grace I have this much faith, that as long as we have been born into his family we have found refuge at his lotus feet. From his lips I have heard that when a man attains illumination, seven generations of his family before and after him become liberated. And the Lord himself was born into our family as a human being! Through his grace and in his holy company we also had many visions and spiritual experiences. Thus he gave us faith and devotion to him.

"In the garden house at Cossipore on that memorable day he touched me as well as others. [This was January 1, 1886, the occasion when Sri Ramakrishna gave unusual spiritual graces to all present.] I feel a thrill whenever I recall the wonderful experience I had as a result of his touch. [About this experience, Ramlal Dada later said: "That day, by his touch, he gave me a clear vision of my Chosen Ideal."] And the absorption he gave me when I would sing *kirtan* with him is beyond expression. He who knows, knows. The Master used to say (referring to himself and his intimate disciples): 'The party of minstrels came and went; nobody recognized them.'

"He was a rare soul. He exemplified the virtue of giving honor to all. Whenever he asked us to do the smallest thing, out of consideration he would ask with great hesitancy."

Maharaj: "Well, brother, at the beginning we did not understand the Master either. Often we were disrespectful to him. But he is the ocean of unconditional grace. He has forgiven our many faults and has made us his own by his love and affection.

"In those days I was very proud and used to lose

my temper over trifling things. The Master said to me: 'Anger is demonic. Pride and anger are great obstacles on the spiritual path. You have come here to live a holy life. Give up anger and envy!'

"In him alone we found our mother, our father, our brother, our friend, our everything." Maharaj folded his hands and chanted the verse: "Thou art my mother and father. Thou art my friend and constant companion. Thou art my wisdom and my wealth. Thou art all-in-all, my God of gods."

Maharaj closed his eyes. After a while he said: "There has never come to earth another who was such an ocean of boundless grace. Those who have understood this truth, and those whom he made understand through his grace, they alone can know and understand him. Blessed are they! (He quoted Hanuman's words to Rama's sons.) 'O Kusha and Lava, why are you proud? If I did not let myself be caught, could you ever catch me?'

"Sri Ramakrishna is attached to his devotees. The breeze of his grace is blowing. Take a little trouble to set your sail. Then the touch of that breeze of grace will make your boat of life land at his feet.

"The Master spoke frequently about self-effort and earnestness. Without enthusiasm and self-effort nothing can be achieved in spiritual life. He would say: 'I have cooked and placed the food before you. Now you must use your hand to put the food into your mouth.' This much exertion is needed.

"Pray to the Lord with all your heart! Then alone

you will long for him. When one is hungry one enjoys food. When one has no appetite one doesn't care even for delicacies. And that is why people don't taste the nectar of his name.

"Now that a little of your mind goes toward the Lord, apply your mind and practice. As you practice, you will receive help. The Master used to say: 'The Mother supplies from her storehouse of knowledge.' If you want to feel the heat of a fire, it won't do to stay too far away. You have to get closer to the fire in order to feel the heat.

"Keep association with the holy. Go to one who knows the path, learn about the path, and walk on the path. Then alone you will reach your destination some day. Then alone will arise faith and devotion."

Ramlal Dada said good-bye; he was about to return to Dakshineswar. We prostrated before Maharaj and Ramlal Dada, and meditating on their entrancing words and on the boundless grace of Sri Ramakrishna we left Balaram Mandir.

ONCE AGAIN I WENT to Balaram Mandir to visit Maharaj. In the course of conversation the subject of our Mission work came up. Maharaj said: "If one works unselfishly, without desiring the fruits of action, work does not create any bondage. Swamiji used to say: 'Work is worship.' Is it possible for everybody to meditate all the time? That is why Swamiji taught selfless service in order to make it easy for people to reach union with God. Know that all work is the

Lord's work. Learn to forget yourself while working. The aim of all spiritual practice is to destroy the sense of ego. Sri Ramakrishna used to say: 'When the ego dies all troubles cease.' As long as we are egotistic, so long is He at a distance. The Master used to give this illustration: 'As long as the manager is in the store-room, the head of the house does not go there. If anybody asks something of him, he directs that person to the manager.'

"Work, devotion, discrimination—each one is a path to reach union with God. With the same whole-souled devotion with which a devotee worships the Lord in the shrine he must serve the Lord in the poor, in the sick, in the lowly. Who are you to help another? It is only when the Lord gives you the power that you can really serve.

"True it is that in all creatures He dwells, but His greater manifestation is in man. That is why Swamiji encouraged us to serve mankind. One must have faith that the one Brahman is in man, woman, in all creatures; and with that faith one must learn to serve Shiva in the form of jiva. As you practice this, suddenly one day the veil will be lifted and you will see that it is He who has become everything—man and universe. It is He who pervades the universe in so many forms. You are that all-pervading Shiva; and thus can serve Shiva in the form of jiva.

"Once the Master asked Mani Mallik's daughter: 'Whom do you love the most?' She replied: 'I have a nephew; I love him the most.' The Master told her:

'Very good! Serve your nephew, bathe him and feed him as Baby Krishna.' She followed the Master's advice and in course of time she had the vision of Baby Krishna in the nephew.

"Practice any spiritual discipline with faith and devotion; in the end it will lead you to the same goal."

AFTER ABOUT A WEEK, I went to the Udbodhan and prostrated before Swami Saradananda. A young swami was asking his advice about some work. Swami Saradananda gave his opinion and then said: "Go to Balaram Mandir and ask Maharaj about it. Maharaj's word is the Master's word. Whatever Maharaj says to us we consider as coming directly from Sri Ramakrishna. The Master and his spiritual son are one and the same."

We went to Balaram Mandir. Maharaj was seated in the living room surrounded by many devotees. His eyes were half-closed. After some time he said: "What is the aim of spiritual practice? To know Him, to attain union with Him. Through His grace 'the knot of the heart, which is ignorance is loosed, all doubts are dissolved, all evil effects of deeds are destroyed, when He who is both personal and impersonal is realized.' Take refuge in Him and earnestly pray for His grace. Why did you come here, renouncing hearth and home? While eating, while lying down, while standing, while sitting, pray to Him: 'Lord, give me the power to feel and understand your grace!'

"We are only travelers in this world. Our eternal abode is at the lotus feet of God. Sri Krishna said in the Gita: 'I am the end of the path, the witness, the Lord, the sustainer. I am the place of abode, the beginning, the friend, and the refuge. I am the breaking-apart and the storehouse of life's dissolution. I lie under the seen, of all creatures the seed that is changeless.'

"Unfortunate is he who, instead of taking refuge in God, becomes entangled in the world. The blessed feet of the Lord are our eternal home. We must reach them somehow. He alone is the truth. That truth is to be attained. Let not your life pass by in vain. Almost everyone thinks that what he understands is the truth and the way for everybody. Sometimes man becomes so egotistic and thinks himself so important that he does not even accept the existence of God. It is this ego that binds a man in maya. There is no escape until you begin to feel, 'Not I, not I, but Thou, my Lord!'

"Swamiji used to sing this song:

> Thou art my Lord,
> Thou art my Master,
> I am Thy servant,
> I am Thy slave.

"Again he would sing: 'All that exists art Thou.' Only he knows God on whom His grace descends. Never forget that the ideal is to know Him. Know Him, and the door to infinite wisdom opens. Then is it that one really feels: 'God is my own; I belong to him.'

"Sri Krishna said in the Gita: 'Lay down all duties in Me, your refuge. Fear no longer, for I will save you from sin and from bondage.' This is His promise. 'Give Me your whole heart. Love and adore Me. Worship Me always. Bow to Me only, and you shall find Me!'

"The Master repeatedly prayed: 'Thou art my refuge, O Lord. I seek no physical pleasures. I do not want worldly happiness. Give me faith, and give me pure love for thy lotus feet. Destroy my sense of ego and make me thine.'

"In this age there is no way other than that of taking shelter at His feet. In the Iron Age, man's span of life is short. And within this short span of life one has to attain Him. There is no time for severe austerities as in olden days. The mind is weak. That is why man is more attached to worldly pleasures.

"In spite of all weakness, the easiest way to attain God is to take refuge in him. What does this mean? Shall we not do anything? Shall we remain passive? No! We must pray; we must cry unto God that he may awaken in us longing for him and that our cravings for enjoyment may be wiped out. Pray: 'O Lord of the Universe, reveal your grace to me! I am helpless. I have no shelter but you. You are the only refuge of the weak. Give me strength to remember you always.' If one can really surrender oneself to God, then everything becomes easy; but it is not so easy to do this. Without divine grace it is not possible to take refuge in God. And in order to feel this grace one must associate with holy men, read sacred books, and pray earnestly.

"The mind deludes us in many ways. We must control it and direct it along the right path. What is austerity? It is to direct the mind toward God in order to taste divine bliss. In this age it is not necessary to practice physical austerities, such as standing on your head. The path in this age is to create the desire to chant the Lord's name, to be compassionate toward all beings, and to serve holy men. The sage Narada attained devotion and knowledge of Brahman by serving holy men. Ego is destroyed through service.

"Sri Ramakrishna's message in this age is renunciation of lust and gold. You have joined the monastery in order to become holy men. Renunciation of lust and gold is the ornament of a holy man, and it is the only means of attaining God. As one progresses on the path of spirituality, one is confronted by many kinds of temptations. Cravings—such as for woman and gold, for name and fame—arise again and may lead one farther away from God. Unless you beware of this thief in the form of cravings he will steal all the goodness in you, and you will drown in the bottomless ocean of worldliness. But, on the other hand, there is the ocean of divine grace—if anyone will sincerely call on Him but once. The Master used to say: 'If you move one step toward Him, He comes down ten steps toward you.'

"God is the wish-yielding tree. He fulfills the heart's desire of his devotee. Be sincere; make your mind and lips the same. There is no injustice in God's kingdom. The Master told us: 'I have done one hundred percent. You do one percent.' What hard austerities the Master practiced in order that our path might be easy! Make him your refuge. Be an heir to immortal bliss in this very life. Make your human birth blessed!"

ANOTHER DAY, MAHARAJ asked Baradananda to sing several songs. After the music, Maharaj said: "Blessed is he in whose heart a current of joy flows continually while he chants the name and sings the praises of the Lord. Keep recollectedness of God and make your life blessed; otherwise, vain is this human birth. 'O Lord, your children are almost dead— deluded by your maya. Give them your life-giving medicine, and make them immortal.' You have left hearth and home. Now forget physical comforts, and pray: 'Lord, thou art my all in all, my support and my only treasure.'"

SWAMI SATPRAKASHANANDA

IT WAS IN FEBRUARY 1910, as far as I remember, that I saw Maharaj for the first time. Having been associated with the ideals and activities of the Ramakrishna Order from my boyhood, I had long cherished a desire to visit at the earliest opportunity

Dakshineswar, Belur Math, and such personalities as the Holy Mother, Maharaj, and M., the recorder of the *Gospel of Sri Ramakrishna*. With this object in view I came to Calcutta from my home town. I had already visited the Holy Mother and M. a day or two before. It was on the day of the Saraswati Puja, the worship of the Goddess of Knowledge, that I crossed the Ganges and went to Belur Math on a ferryboat. As I walked along the grassy lawn toward the old residential building of the monastery, I noticed that Maharaj was seated on the open terrace, facing the gate. Thus he was the first person I saw on my first visit to the monastery. I would have considered it a coincidence had I not been told in later years that Swami Prabhavananda and Swami Akhilananda had similar experiences.

I bowed to Maharaj and took the dust of his feet. He very affectionately asked me in a sweet voice where I had come from and where I lived. I told him I lived very close to the house where Swami Vivekananda had stayed when he visited our home town.

The second time I saw Maharaj was in December 1911. Although I had been closely associated with the Ramakrishna Order and had great admiration for the monastic life, I did not yet know if I could ever be a monk. Each time I came to Maharaj he made some remark which confirmed my belief that he already knew the future course of my life. He told me: "You should come here as often as you can. You will not be the loser."

For several years I could not see Maharaj because whenever I came to Belur Math he was away. Meanwhile I became well acquainted with Swami Premananda. One day at Dacca, Swami Premananda introduced me to Maharaj, saying: "This boy has been trying to secure a plot of land for our Order."

Maharaj remarked: "I know him."

Swami Premananda said: "How? You were not at the monastery when he came."

Then I said: "I met Maharaj some years ago."

Maharaj turned to me and asked: "Can you find a place for us?" I did not understand what he meant. He repeated the question. I told him: "It is all for you, Maharaj." He simply smiled. I did not know then that he was asking me whether I had a place for him in my heart. This is one example of how even in ordinary conversation his words had much deeper significance than we realized at the time.

On one occasion Maharaj said: "Continue your spiritual practice in the way you are doing." From my early youth I used to sit regularly every day for meditation. I did not know whether I was gaining anything from it or whether I was proceeding correctly. I had not told Maharaj anything about it. Therefore his remark made a tremendous impression on me. How had he known? I had not even asked him for spiritual instruction. Several times he told me: "Do not be impatient." I wondered what he meant because it did not seem to me that I was. Later, when I asked him for spiritual advice, he gave me preliminary instructions, saying: "You will have a new life." Actually, I felt that a light was kindled within me which has burned ever since. Gradually it seemed that the spiritual treasure house was unlocked and the entire spiritual realm became an open book.

It was not until 1916 that I made the decision to enter the monastic life. I asked Maharaj for approval. He said: "As long as your mother is alive you should not leave her. She has no one else to look after her. You should serve her. Just practice truthfulness and continence." He did not prescribe any further rules or regulations for me.

When Maharaj initiated me I asked him: "What relationship shall I maintain with my Chosen Ideal?" He said: "This will develop within you as you follow the spiritual course. . . . He is your all in all." Then I asked him the meaning of the mantram. He said: "There is no difference in meaning between the mantram and the Chosen Ideal. They mean the same thing. He is your all in all." The one thing that Maharaj urged was the steady and persistent practice of the instruction he gave me. Twice he prescribed for me *purascharan.*

Maharaj hardly spoke about himself or Sri Ramakrishna. One day at Balaram Bose's house a lay devotee, Lalit Babu, pointed to a wall painting of Sri Ramakrishna and asked Maharaj: "Was the Master like this?" Maharaj looked at the picture and became very grave, as if his thoughts were too deep for words.

HOLY PLACES had a special attraction for Maharaj. I spent memorable days with him in the Advaita Ashrama in Benares. Maharaj seemed to be in the happiest mood there. From time to time he spoke highly of the spiritual atmosphere of the place. There were continuous festivity, worship, and devotional singing and dancing.

Every morning we used to assemble in Maharaj's room for meditation. In the evenings all the swamis met there and asked questions. Maharaj would answer them. There were lively discussions. One day I was late in arriving. The whole room was full. I tried to secure a seat among the swamis. As I turned from one to another, Maharaj jokingly remarked: "First trace, then you can write. You have to go through preliminary exercises to enter the fold." All laughed.

One day in Benares I asked Maharaj: "I do not feel any love for God, nor do I feel any attachment to the world. Does this mean that I have bad tendencies within me?" Maharaj said: "You don't have to worry about that."

Maharaj always treated me very affectionately. Once Lalit Babu wanted me to collect funds for the temple at the Holy Mother's birthplace. But Maharaj did not approve of it. He thought it would be too hard a task for me. It was not often that I brought any present to Maharaj. But whenever I took any offering to him, he accepted it very graciously, with deep appreciation. Even when I made blunders he was unperturbed. On one occasion I made a bad mistake

which would have offended any other spiritual
teacher. But Maharaj was exceedingly gracious. In
Maharaj I found for the first time a person who could
love others, not in spite of, but with all their faults.
His love drew me, and I could not get away. He could
hardly brook any criticism of his disciples by others.

One day I came to see Maharaj at Balaram Bose's
house and found him seated in the living room after
the noontime siesta. Just then Golap-Ma, a disciple
of Sri Ramakrishna and companion of the Holy
Mother, came to the room. She was relating how a lay
devotee had held a special worship in his home to
which he had invited some of the swamis and had
given presents to them. Then she remarked: "Although he is serving the swamis with great devotion,
his character is not changing." Maharaj became very
grave and said: "Golap-Ma, you don't understand."

Sometimes Maharaj made fun at the expense of
Swami Akhandananda and other brother-disciples
and asked me to assist him. But his eyes and face
always bore an expression of inner serenity and pro-
fundity.

His brother-disciples held Maharaj in great reverence. One day Swami Saradananda came to Maharaj's room at the Udbodhan Office to report on Swami
Turiyananda, who was ill at the time and staying
upstairs. Swami Saradananda was standing beside the
cot on which Maharaj was seated. Maharaj asked him
to sit by him, but Swami Saradananda kept standing.
When Maharaj repeated the request, Swami Sarada-

nanda, as if in obedience to his wish, picked up the corner of the mattress and sat on the bare cot. He did not think himself worthy of sitting on the same mattress as Maharaj.

One day Swami Dhirananda told Maharaj about me: "He has some questions to ask." Maharaj turned to me and said: "You have seen a holy man, you have bowed to him, you have touched his feet. What more questions can there be?"

I used to read the Bhagavad-Gita and the Upanishads before I came to Maharaj. But it was only after I received his grace that I could absorb the true spirit of the scriptures. Though I studied hard before, I had not understood the real significance of the words. But later, everything became clear to me, and I felt that it was all through the grace of Maharaj. He did not talk much on religion but transmitted spirituality in silence. He was the very embodiment of love and compassion. His unconditional grace is my only resource.

SWAMI OMKARESWARANANDA

IT WAS THE EVENING of March 14, 1916, the day following the public celebration of Sri Ramakrishna's birthday. Swami Premananda and Swami Akhandananda were seated on a bench on the eastern veranda of the Belur Monastery, overlooking the Ganges. Several other swamis and young brahmacharis were seated on a bench nearby. Presently Swami

Achalananda, who was one of the group, addressed Swami Premananda:

"Revered Sir, please tell us something about Sri Ramakrishna. To hear of him directly from you is far more inspiring and uplifting than to read of him and his teachings in the Gospel."

"Very little of the Master's teachings is recorded in the Gospel," replied the Swami. "There is too much repetition. M. used to visit the Master occasionally and would note down his teachings as he heard them. But Sri Ramakrishna taught his disciples differently, according to their different temperaments and their capacity of understanding. His teachings to the monastic disciples were given in private. As soon as the householder disciples would leave the room he would get up and lock the door and then speak to us living words of renunciation. He would try to impress upon our young minds the emptiness and vanity of worldly enjoyments. In his great mercy he would point out to us how dry and hot the world is—like a desert; and how, like a mirage, it burns the heart but never slakes the thirst. He taught us how to discriminate and analyze the body of man, made up as it is of flesh, blood, and bones, etc., so that our minds would not run after the enjoyments of the flesh. He would tell us of the great power of the all-bewitching maya, and how man, forgetting his divine heritage, falls ever and again into her clutches. Deep down within his heart man knows full well that there is no lasting happiness to be found in the mad pursuit of worldly enjoyments, and yet, like the camel who chews thorny bushes even while his mouth bleeds, so man still stirs up his lust for enjoyment even while he suffers. To satisfy his lust man needs gold. Lust and gold! These are the chains that drag a man down to the pit of worldliness. He alone soars high who shakes himself free of these chains. He who renounces sexual appetites—not in conduct only, but also in thought—he it is who has renounced all worldly pleasures. He alone is a man of true renunciation. Renunciation is not in the garb of a monk, nor is it in the renunciation of fish and meat.

"Spiritual aspirants of many different sects would come to visit Sri Ramakrishna at Dakshineswar, and all of them found great satisfaction in talking to him. To each he was able to show the way to further progress along his own particular path, so that each thought that the Master was a perfected soul of his own particular sect. They could not know that Sri Ramakrishna was as broad as the sky and as deep as the ocean, and thoroughly acquainted with all the different sects and paths. For he had followed them each in turn, and by each path he had reached the same goal.

"Never forget that the ideal of life is to realize God, to see God. You have renounced the world to reach that goal. Struggle hard to grow in love for him. Attain him. He is the very life of our life, the soul of our soul. He is the Lord of our heart, he is our very own. Yearn for him with a longing heart. How blessed you are that you have the privilege of serving and associating with such ever-free souls as Swami Brahmananda and others who are the associates of God incarnate! Do not neglect this opportunity. You are men! Be gods! Teach others by the example of your own lives."

Swami Premananda remained silent for a while, then continued:

"I see very clearly that, after we are gone, multitudes will come to learn from you young men."

A young swami: "But, revered Sir, how can that be? If multitudes are to come, they should come while you are still living."

Swami Premananda replied: "Do not think that you are any less great than we! You have received the grace of the Holy Mother. Do you think we have become great just because people have come to take the dust of our feet? No! We first saw Sri Ramakrishna and then renounced the world; you are great indeed because you have renounced the world without seeing him!"

Young Swami: "But revered Sir, Sri Ramakrishna made you great."

Swami Premananda: "No! Sri Ramakrishna did not make us great; he made us 'nobodies.' You also have to become 'nobodies.' Wipe out all vanity and all sense of ego. Sri Ramakrishna used to say, 'When the ego dies, all troubles cease.' 'Not I, not I, but thou, O Lord.' Look at the life of Nag Mahasaya! There was not the least trace of ego in him. G. C. Ghosh used to say, 'Maya tried to bind Nag Mahasaya and Vivekananda in her net, but Nag Mahasaya became smaller than the smallest, so that maya's net could not hold him, and Vivekananda grew bigger and bigger; he became one with the infinite, and the net was too small to bind him.'

"Do you know of what this net of maya is comprised? Sense objects, lust, gold, name, fame, ego, vanity, selfishness, and so on. With all these, maya binds the mind of man. Come out of this net, and the mind will run straight to God. All bondage is in the mind. All freedom is in the mind.

"The worldly man is drunk with the objects of sense, with name, with fame, with lust, with gold. Be you also drunk, but be drunk with selfless works, with love of God, with ecstasy, with samadhi!"

Swami Brahmananda now came and sat silently beside Swami Premananda. Swami Shivananda followed and sat on a bench facing them. Many young swamis and brahmacharis—about sixty altogether, came and sat around the swamis. In the presence of Swami Brahmananda, the spiritual son and most beloved disciple of Sri Ramakrishna, the minds of all were filled with joy; they became lost in contemplation. Stillness reigned within their hearts; all nature seemed to stand still, while the Ganges flowed silently by.

Some time passed in that great silence, until, after a while, it was broken by a remark about the well-known Shankara Monastery at Puri and the abbots connected with it. Then, as the conversation drifted from one subject to another, Swami Brahmananda said: "Once, when I was at Puri I met a holy man whose name was Ranga Swami. He was about ninety-five years old, and a man of great renunciation. He was always drunk with the love of God. He would eat only that which had first been offered in the temple. At one time he was very ill, and I wanted to give him some medicine, but he refused to take it. Knowing his habit I arranged with the priest of the temple to offer some milk to the deity, and with that I mixed the medicine which the Swami took as sacramental food."

In the course of conversation a well-known writer and preacher was mentioned.

Swami Shivananda: "But what can he know about religion? He is steeped in worldliness. He who does not live the life of renunciation cannot be a teacher. Dispassion is the first principle of spiritual life. A man of learning may write books or give lectures, but if he has no dispassion in his heart and if he does not practice what he teaches, his words cannot be effective for they have no power behind them. They merely create a momentary sensation.

"The other day I learned that a certain teacher of the Brahmo Samaj was complaining that more people were coming to the Belur Math and fewer to the Brahmo Samaj, and that someone had suggested that they introduce a girls' choir to attract the people. When the revered Shivanath Shastri heard this he remarked that if the Brahmos would incorporate into their lives more of the dispassion and renunciation of the monks of Belur Math they too would attract people."

Swami Brahmananda: "Shivanath Shastri is a sincere soul and has a great regard for truth. He is earnest in his desire to realize God. He is living now at Bhubaneswar and is practicing spiritual disciplines. He already has some inner awakening. After all, he had the blessed good fortune to associate with our master. Bijoy Goswami was another great spiritual leader in the Brahmo Samaj, and it was a great loss to the Samaj when he left it."

Swami Shivananda: "One day Swamiji, Swami Akhandananda, and I were traveling on the river Ganges. Swamiji was speaking very highly of Devendra Nath Tagore, when all at once we noticed the Maharshi's yacht at some distance from us. We approached nearer to pay our respects to the Maharshi, who, when he learned that we were disciples of Sri Ramakrishna, seemed very happy to meet us and repeatedly remarked: 'Ah! how great is the love of Sri Ramakrishna! How great is his devotion!' The Maharshi then asked Swamiji to recite some passages from the Upanishads, which he did. After listening for some time he said, 'I understand and appreciate the devotional passages in the Upanishads; I do not care for the nondualistic ideas.'"

After listening to the discussions for some time, Swami Premananda remarked: "When Shivanath

Shastri or some other of the learned members of the Brahmo Samaj would visit Sri Ramakrishna, he would sometimes become just like a child and ask them: 'Is my condition really like that of one who is mad? Tell me, have I gone crazy thinking of God?' And indeed, there were some who really did think that our master was a madman!"

Swami Brahmananda: "Only a jeweler can know the value of a jewel. There was once a poor man who found a diamond. He had no idea of its value, so he took it to the vegetable market to have it appraised. The vegetable man looked at it and then offered him five cents worth of vegetables for it, but the poor man thought it was worth twenty cents. Upon being refused, he took it to a rice merchant who offered him one bag of rice, but he wanted four bags. Next he went to a goldsmith, and he was offered a hundred rupees. This offer aroused the greed in the man, and he began to realize that the diamond was really valuable, so he took it to a jeweler who offered him twenty thousand rupees. Even this did not satisfy him, so he took it to the finest jeweler in the city. As soon as the jeweler saw it he realized its real worth and immediately offered him a million rupees. And that is how it goes. A holy man is judged according to the worth and capacity of the appraiser. By some Sri Ramakrishna was regarded as a holy man, by others as a madman. But those who knew saw in him the manifest incarnation of God."

TARA

I WAS PRACTICALLY BROUGHT UP in the theater. Ever since I was a little girl I worked on the stage with Girish Chandra Ghosh and heard from him about Sri Ramakrishna. There was a photograph of Sri Ramakrishna in every theater with which Girish Babu was connected, and the actors and actresses used to bow down to the Master's photograph before they appeared on the stage. I think this has now become a custom in every Bengali theater.

Many a time I wanted to visit the Belur Math. Once I asked Girish Babu if he would let me attend a particular celebration. I recall his answer perfectly. He said: "Not yet. When the Lord wills, you will go." And so, in spite of my wish, I did not then visit the monastery.

My first visit to the Belur Math took place many years later (about 1916). I was then depressed and restless; life seemed unbearable to me. I began to seek out places of pilgrimage. In this unhappy state of mind I finally went to the Belur Math. Binodini, the finest actress of Bengal at the time, was with me. When I was seven years old she introduced me to the theater; and again it was she who introduced me to the monastery.

It was past noon when we came to the Math. Maharaj had finished his midday meal and was about to go to his room to rest. At that moment we arrived and prostrated before him.

Maharaj said: "Hello Binode! Hello Tara! So you have come! You are too late; we have already finished our lunch. You should have let us know that you were coming."

We could see how worried he was about us. He immediately ordered fruit to be brought which had been offered to the Lord. And arrangements were made to fry *luchis* for us. We went first to the shrine, then had our *prasad*, and afterward were shown around the Math by a swami. Maharaj did not have his rest that day.

We were brought up to revere holy men. But along with respect and faith I felt much fear of them. I was impure—a fallen woman. And so when I touched the holy feet of Maharaj I did it with great hesitancy, afraid to offend him. But his sweet words, his solicitude and love dispelled all my fear.

Maharaj asked me: "Why don't you come here often?"

I replied: "I was afraid to come to the Math."

Maharaj said with great earnestness: "Fear? You are coming to Sri Ramakrishna. What fear can there be? We all of us are his children. Don't be afraid! Whenever you wish, come here. Daughter, the Lord does not care about externals; he sees our inmost heart. There should be no fear in approaching him."

Swami Premananda was there at the time. He also

was very gracious to us. He remarked: "The Lord welcomes everybody."

I had tea at the monastery in the afternoon and then returned home. When I said good-bye to Maharaj he told me: "Come here often. You were inconvenienced today. Come another time and take the regular prasad."

This was my first visit to Maharaj—and this was the first time in my life I received genuine love.

A few days later, Maharaj went to the theater to see the play *Ramanuja*. [Tara took the part of Ramanuja, the famous philosopher, as a young boy.] After the performance I took the dust of Maharaj's feet. Maharaj blessed me and said: "Very good! May you grow in devotion!"

The days passed. I was restless as before—burning within. I could find no refuge, no peace anywhere. Everything seemed empty, empty! I started on a pilgrimage to Puri, longing to see Lord Jagannath (the image of the Lord of the Universe in the famous temple). On my way I stopped at an inn at Bhubaneswar. There I learned that Maharaj was then staying at the Bhubaneswar monastery. So I went to visit him.

He welcomed me with the same solicitude and affection as before. He said: "Oh, you look so tired! Why did you come in this hot sun? Where do you take your meals? From tomorrow on come to the Math for prasad every day. What do you like to eat? Well, daughter, of course you realize that we are monks and can't provide a feast, and delicacies can't be had in this little town."

In this vein Maharaj spoke to me. I was surprised. What kind of a holy man was this? A worldly man would not feel such concern for his sons and daughters. Who was I? Where was my place in society? Down—down below! I had nothing to expect from the world but hatred and indifference. I had no friend, no relative. This big world seemed to me like a stranger's house. Nobody talked to me without a selfish motive; nobody looked at me without a selfish desire. There was none in this world whom I could call my own. Until today!

Swami Brahmananda, the spiritual son of Sri Ramakrishna, the all-renouncing monk, revered and respected by all—that is Maharaj. And with what undeserved care and affection he made me his own! I never saw my father, he died before I was born. I thought to myself: "Is this what a father's affection is like? Or is this something greater?"

I could not hold back my tears. My lifelong sorrow melted as the tears fell from my eyes, and I realized: Here is my refuge. Here is someone to whom I am not a sinner, I am not an outcast.

I am the daughter of Maharaj. He who has none is Maharaj's own. He is my Maharaj—my father, my heaven, my peace, my God.

What peace I found! Maharaj said many things— I can't remember them all. But what I remember is my treasure in this life. He said: "Daughter, you know what suffering there is in this world. Don't think that we have not experienced any suffering. When I came to Sri Ramakrishna I was a young boy. I was practicing spiritual disciplines, but my mind was not always tranquil. I was restless, and there was the attraction of the world. At times I thought that my life was in vain, for I found no peace.

"One day I was thinking along these lines. I decided that I would run away and not even say good-bye to the Master—when suddenly I found him standing before me. He said: 'What are you worrying about?' He placed his hand on my head and blessed me. Where was suffering then? What bliss, what bliss!"

I burst out: "Father, my suffering is great! I cannot bear any more! I run restlessly here and there. Take away this suffering of mine as Sri Ramakrishna took away yours!"

In a tender, affectionate voice Maharaj said: "Call on Sri Ramakrishna. He was born for this purpose. You have nothing to fear. Chant his name. For a few days it will be difficult; then he will do everything for you. Have no more fear. You will realize great bliss. You will know what fun life can be."

We had read in books how Sri Chaitanya and Nityananda came to earth to save the fallen ones. Today I have had such an experience for myself—the infinite grace of Maharaj—as if Maharaj had come for sinners like me.

"There is nothing to fear, daughter. What fear can

there be for the Lord's children?" What words of
hope! What consolation! Maharaj seems to be ex-
tending his arms to us, saying: "Come all ye fallen
ones! Come all ye who are suffering! Take refuge in
the Lord! He *is!* Have no fear!"

May it please the Lord that I will never forget, not
even in death, these words of consolation!

SWAMI VIJNANANANDA

ANYONE COMING INTO THE ORBIT of Swamiji (Swami
Vivekananda) and Maharaj could feel a special
spiritual atmosphere. Whosoever entered into that
orbit could feel at once a power permeating him.

Swamiji loved us, his brother disciples, intensely. It
was like a mother's love for her child, and so he could
not brook faults or defects in any of us. He wanted
his brothers to be as great as he himself was—no,
even greater than he. There is no love equal to his
love for us. But he had a very special love for Maharaj, and respect for him. There is a saying: "The
guru's son is to be respected as the guru himself."
That was Swamiji's attitude toward Maharaj. I lived
in the shade of Maharaj's protection and so I did not
receive much of Swamiji's scolding. Maharaj and
Swami Premananda chose to bear most of the burden
of it.

One time I did not get the meaning of something
Swamiji said and contradicted him: "No, holy sir,
you have not understood the ancient sages and

seers." I saw Swamiji's face turning red. Maharaj was walking back and forth near us. Swamiji told him: "Raja, look here. This fellow says I don't understand anything." Maharaj replied: "Brother, you should not take seriously what he says. He is just a young boy. What does he know?" Swamiji immediately calmed down. He accepted Maharaj's words as if he himself were a child. And Swamiji and I were reconciled.

Because Swamiji loved Maharaj with such intensity, he once scolded him so vehemently that Maharaj went to his room and wept copiously. I must mention that the fault was mine. In order to shield me Maharaj took the blame upon himself. When Swamiji learned that Maharaj was weeping, he became so upset that he rushed into Maharaj's room and after embracing him began to weep too, and said: "Raja, Raja, please, brother, forgive me. How wrong I was to have scolded you!" Seeing Swamiji weep like this, Maharaj was struck with wonder and said: "Well, you have scolded me. What of it? You scolded me because you love me." Swamiji again embraced Maharaj and repeated over and over again: "Brother, please forgive me. Our master loved you so much. He never spoke a harsh word to you. And over a trifling matter I scolded you." He spoke in this way for a long time, and then they both became calm.

I will never forget that experience. I have seen with my own eyes what powerful attraction these two great souls Maharaj and Swamiji had for spiritual aspirants. People could not help but be drawn to them.

SWAMI VISHUDDHANANDA

I WAS WITH MAHARAJ in Benares. One day we went to the temple of Vishwanath. There were many other persons in the party. As he entered the temple, Maharaj saw a sweeper cleaning the compound. Maharaj took the broomstick from the man's hand and began to sweep the place himself. We felt he was showing us that if one goes to a temple to see the deity one must have this attitude of humility. Seeing Maharaj's example, one of the devotees also began to sweep. But it seemed artificial. What Maharaj did was natural; it looked so beautiful and was so inspiring!

On one occasion, in the house of Balaram Bose, Maharaj said: "You practice meditation and japam; you progress a little, then comes a period of dryness. It seems that the doors are entirely closed. At that time it is necessary that you stick to your spiritual practices with infinite patience; by so doing you will find one day that all of a sudden the doors are opened. What a great joy it is then! In spiritual life many such thresholds have to be crossed."

Once Maharaj said to a devotee: "When you meditate, you should imagine that God is standing before you like the mythical wish-fulfilling tree." Another day he said to the same devotee: "At the time of meditation you should imagine that you are in mid-ocean, on all sides there are mountain-high waves, and God is standing before you ready to help you."

In Madras, while I accompanied him on a walk, Maharaj said to me, "Just do one thing: always try to remember God. I also do that."

In Benares Maharaj once severely scolded a senior member of the Sevashrama there for committing a blunder. Afterward I asked Maharaj: "If you become so displeased with us for our faults, what shall we do? You know we are weak and therefore are liable to make mistakes." At this, Maharaj bit his lip and said: "All these things—like my becoming angry—are from the lips (touching his lips) and not from within (touching his heart)."

Once I was massaging Maharaj for a long time. I was tired and felt I could continue no longer. Still I did not dare say I was tired. All of a sudden it occurred to me: Had I been in the world I would have had to work so hard, and instead I have the opportunity and privilege to serve Maharaj and I feel tired! As soon as this thought came to my mind, all fatigue vanished. I felt great strength within. I began to massage Maharaj with doubled enthusiasm. Just at that moment a strange thing happened. Maharaj said to me: "All right, that's enough. You need not massage me any longer." Maharaj could read the hearts of people. He had been testing me.

SWAMI ASESHANANDA

THE YEAR 1922 is a memorable year in my life. On Sri Ramakrishna's birthday that year I was initiated into brahmacharya by Maharaj. I had been staying at the Udbodhan Office in Calcutta as the attendant of Swami Saradananda. With Swami Saradananda's permission I went to visit Belur Math for several days. When I approached Maharaj for brahmacharya, he said with a very sober face: "Swami Saradananda is very rich! You are his attendant. You must pay me one hundred and eight rupees as my fee. Otherwise I can't initiate you."

Stunned, I replied: "Maharaj, I have no money. It is impossible for me to pay such a large amount. If you don't bless me, I am lost."

Then Maharaj said gravely: "I have a suggestion that will solve your problem. Go to Swami Saradananda and ask him to pay that amount for you."

I gave the message to Swami Saradananda. With great seriousness he dictated a letter to Maharaj, which he signed and asked me to deliver. The letter read: "Revered Maharaj, I am yours and everything in Udbodhan belongs to you. Whatever you ask for will be given immediately."

I had my brahmacharya initiation. Of course, no money was paid; it was all in fun. A man who is established in samadhi likes to play. He imitates the Lord in his divine sport. He enjoys the fun because he is desireless, whereas we take everything seriously and suffer because we are involved in maya.

This incident was very meaningful to me; it brought me closer to Maharaj. Previously I had gone to him and bowed down with reverence, but there had been a feeling of awe and hesitance. Maharaj, as a great teacher, knew that the sense of awe and aloof-ness is an obstacle to spiritual growth. It is through nearness and love that barriers are annihilated and intimate relationships established. Since that day I felt free with Maharaj and went to his room for my morning meditations. It was a delight to watch Maha-raj's face. There would be perfect silence, and Maha-raj would be completely absorbed. In his presence the mind automatically calmed down and tranquillity filled the heart. I remembered the words of Sri Ramakrishna and felt how true they were: "If you sit by a fire, you are bound to get warmth. Similarly, if you associate with an illumined soul you are sure to get spiritual upliftment and joy."

After meditation Maharaj used to come to the veranda overlooking the Ganges and sit in an easy chair. Sometimes there would be songs, at other times talks on various subjects. Once Maharaj said: "Pray to the Lord with a yearning heart. Tell him freely that you desire him alone. Do not doubt that he exists. Those who are meek and lowly are soon blessed with his vision. If you approach him with devotion, he will surely reveal himself. Do not feel shy because you have made mistakes or have not called on him for a long time. He is the very embodi-ment of compassion. He does not care about your faults. Go to him with the simplicity of a child, and he will receive you. Be simple and guileless. Without simplicity and childlike faith nobody can realize him."

Another day Maharaj placed special emphasis on

work. He said: "Always remember that through work you are serving the Lord. One can see him with the eye of devotion. If you work with the idea of pleasing men, you will be disappointed. You will find peace and happiness only if you can remember the Lord. If he is pleased, the world is pleased. In favorable or in adverse circumstances, feel that you have none but him and that you are serving him through the faithful discharge of your allotted duties."

Maharaj had the simplicity of a child and the wisdom of a knower of Brahman. One day he put on the mask of a tiger to frighten the grandchildren of Balaram Bose. After the first cry of fear one of the children said: "Oh, it is Maharaj. You can't frighten me!" Then Maharaj removed the mask and took the children on his lap. He gave them some candies which he had asked me to bring. The next moment Maharaj was so absorbed in contemplation that I could not ask him a question for which I had come. He was so grave that I did not dare speak. I sat in silence, prostrated mentally, and left.

We have not even glimpsed the hundredth part of Maharaj's greatness. Only his brother-disciples understood him. Swami Saradananda used to say: "There is no difference between Maharaj and Sri Ramakrishna." Maharaj ruled us all, not by the authority of his position as the president of the Order, but through the compelling power of his love.

BOSHI SEN

MORE THAN FIFTY YEARS AGO I saw Maharaj at the Howrah Railway Station, Calcutta, for the first time. He was returning from Madras with Swami Abhedananda. We students insisted on releasing the horses from his carriage and ourselves pulled it through the streets to its destination. I can still feel his blessing hand on my head as I took the dust of his feet.

The next time I saw Maharaj was in 1910. He had come to visit my guru, Swami Sadananda, at the house in Bosepara Lane. After Swami Sadananda gave up his body in February 1911, I saw Maharaj often, particularly when he came to Calcutta from Belur. Nevertheless, as I was then working with Dr. J. C. Bose, the world-renowned scientist, I was not always free to go to him whenever I liked, and for this reason Maharaj gave me the nickname of "Season Flower."

Any little service, however insignificant, done with real devotion never escaped his recognition. Once I was asked to prepare a chillum of tobacco for him. Three different attendants in turn came to hurry me, but I refused to take the chillum to Maharaj until I was satisfied that it was just right. When Maharaj drew his first puff, he gave me an affectionate blow on the back. "One more chillum like this, and I will give you sannyas!" he said.

On another occasion I had brought a big fish from my home town of Vishnupur for Maharaj, but the train was very late and when I reached Balaram Mandir one of his attendants, seeing my fish, contemptuously ordered: "Take that fish away! A devotee has sent so much fish today that we have already given away about twenty pounds." Crestfallen, I went up to Maharaj. His first words were: "Boshi, what have you brought for me from Vishnupur?" Very lamely I replied: "I brought a fish, Maharaj, but they tell me you will not have any use for it because you have already had to give away a lot of fish today." At once he said: "Vishnupur fish is very good," and called out: "See that Boshi's fish is properly cleaned and cooked." Of course I went home walking on air.

One day he was talking about the practice of spiritual disciplines as I was in the act of massaging him. "Do you think that there is any fixed, catalogued price of so much austerity, so much japam, so much charity, etc., for God-realization? None can force realization out of Him!" This remark suited me to a T, for I was not practicing any sustained spiritual disciplines at the time. Then he went on: "But . . ." (Why this inconvenient "but"? I asked myself.) "But, if you don't keep up a regular spiritual struggle, you will not be able to hold the experience when it comes."

Once Maharaj expressed a desire to see some of Bose's famous experiments showing the sensitivity of plants to external stimuli. When he visited the institute, he watched the experiments we demonstrated for him with great interest. That evening he was still preoccupied with what he had seen in the laboratory. "There was a time," he told me, "when Sri Rama-krishna could not step on the grass but would jump from one bare spot to another to avoid hurting the grass. At that time we simply didn't believe that grass could be sensitive. From what I saw today, I realize how infallibly true his perceptions were." A little later, he added: "Don't give up your science. You will get everything through this."

In April 1922, the terrible news came that Maharaj had cholera. I hurried over to Balaram's house to find out if it was true. I just peeped into his room, and though his back was turned, he immediately asked: "Who is it?" I asked whether I could fan him. "Yes, do," he said. . . . With his permission, I was allowed to join the group who nursed him.

Two days before he gave up his body, he was in a wonderfully ecstatic mood, showering unending blessings on all in the room. For the first time we heard from his own lips who and what he was. This unforgettable scene has been described by his biogra-phers and need not be repeated by me. The blessed-ness we all felt at the time has not diminished in intensity through all these years. He filled each of us to the utmost limit of our capacity.

A DEVOTEE

MYMENSINGH, SATURDAY, JANUARY 22, 1916. When
I came to the office today I learned that Revered
Maharaj had arrived and was staying at the home of
Jiten Dutta. I went immediately to visit Maharaj, as
I was very anxious to have the blessings of his holy
association. Maharaj came out of his room to go for
a stroll. Swami Premananda met him and they began
to walk along the bank of the river. Many devotees
accompanied them, to which Mr. Dutta objected.

Swami Premananda rebuked Mr. Dutta: "Why do
you object? These people want the association of holy
men. That is the greatest thing in life. Only he who
has good karmas can have the association of *sadhus*.
Holy company is very important. You must not stop
these devotees!"

Maharaj to Swami Premananda: "Look, brother!
How beautiful is this open field! How beautiful is the
river! How gently the breeze is blowing! This is a
grand place! All this is kindling my spiritual consciousness." In a state of ecstasy he continued: "It is
good to meditate mornings and evenings in places
like this. The mind becomes purified. The Lord's
name is the only truth; everything else is unreal. To
have faith in Him, to be devoted to Him, to praise His
glories—these are the only duties in life."

SUNDAY, JANUARY 23, 1916. At half past seven in the
morning I arrived at the home of Mr. Dutta with my

friends Ram, Shyam, and Kiran. Maharaj saw us and said: "Come in!" We prostrated and sat down. The maharaja of Susunga was present.

In the course of conversation Maharaj said to the maharaja: "You see, you love music and singing. You must remember that God can also be approached through music. Music is 'sound-Brahman.' This truth is experienced if one meditates." He said these words with such conviction that they created a deep impression in the minds of everyone present.

I said: "Maharaj, my mind is very restless. It becomes difficult to practice japam and meditation. Please tell me—how can I be helped?"

Maharaj: "Wake up early in the morning. Wash yourself, and choose a firm seat. Command your mind in this way: 'Mind, keep still! Let no distractions enter!' With the strength of the intelligent will, keep the mind under control. Soon it will become concentrated. Then no distractions will arise. A man can train horses and elephants and bring them under control; can't he learn to train his own mind?

"There is no need of many teachings. Now meditate on the words I have spoken to you."

Some arrangements for music were made. All prostrated before Maharaj and went to the drawing room to listen to the program. Swami Premananda had been meditating in a room nearby. He came out of the room and asked Biren: "Who was Maharaj instructing?" Biren pointed to me. Swami Premananda looked at me and said: "Blessed you are! Maharaj rarely instructs people. You will understand later. . . ." I prostrated before him and he blessed me.

Biren told Swami Premananda: "Maharaj loves this boy."

Swami Premananda said: "Yes, I know."

After two or three days Maharaj was to leave for Dacca on the evening train. I went to see him in the afternoon. When the time of departure approached, he blessed everyone and got into a carriage. Swami Premananda and Swami Sankarananda went with him. Maharaj and Swami Premananda sat on one side and Swami Sankarananda on the opposite side of the carriage.

Maharaj saw me standing nearby and said to me: "Come with us!"

"Yes, sir," I answered, "I am walking to the railway station."

Maharaj: "No, no! Come in our carriage!"

I was hesitating. Swami Premananda said: "When Maharaj asks you to come, you must obey him. Don't hesitate!"

So I got into the carriage and sat with Swami Sankarananda. I thought to myself: "How many austerities must I have performed in past lives that I may ride in the same carriage with Maharaj! No, no, it is not my austerities, it is Maharaj's infinite grace."

We reached the station. The time for the train's arrival approached. As arranged, my sister came to prostrate before Maharaj.

He said to her: "Daughter, the train is coming. I don't have much time, but I will give you knowledge in one sentence: Read the *Gospel of Sri Ramakrishna* regularly every day. That is enough. You will find in this book the truth of all religions." My sister felt blessed.

The train came. One by one we prostrated before Maharaj and Swami Premananda. Maharaj blessed us all that we might attain pure devotion and pure knowledge.

Teachings

TEACHINGS OF MAHARAJ

Maharaj, how did Sri Ramakrishna look upon mankind? Please tell us something about him.

Sri Ramakrishna saw God in all beings. Seeing his great love for his disciples, Swami Vivekananda once said to him: "You love us all so much. Is it not possible that, because of this love, you too may meet the same fate that Jada Bharat met?"[1] The Master replied: "True, by thinking of matter one becomes like matter. But you must understand that it is the God

[1]Referring to the story in the Bhagavatam (Wisdom of God), which tells of the king who loved his pet deer so intensely, that after his death he himself was reborn as a deer. The moral of the story is: As you think, so you become. Therefore one should not become attached to any object in the world.

Editor's Note: In this section, Swami Brahmananda's responses and teachings appear in Roman. Questions and responses by disciples and devotees are in italics.

within you that I love. If my mind should ever become attached to any one of you as man or woman,
I would at once dismiss all thought of you from my
mind." Because Sri Ramakrishna taught the ideal of
renunciation to his young disciples, he was often
criticized by the worldly-minded, and to such criticism he would answer: "I have no objection to anyone living in the world. Neither do I teach that every
man and woman should renounce lust and greed. I
teach renunciation only to those in whom there is
already some spiritual awakening. I want these young
men to attain first knowledge and discrimination, and
then, if they wish, they may enter into worldly life."
Indeed, to many who came to him he would say:
"First go out into the world. Gather your experiences, and then, when you have become sick of the
world, come to me for the cure." His teachings varied
to suit all temperaments.

When Swami Turiyananda was quite a young lad,
he asked Sri Ramakrishna how he could give up
thoughts of lust. The Master said: "Give up lust? Why
should you give up lust? Instead of trying to give up,
you should increase your lust!" This advice amazed
the young disciple, but he said nothing, and the Master continued: "Direct all your thoughts of lust and
all your passions toward God." Often he would point
to himself and say: "Everything will be achieved if
you will love *this*. The more intensely you yearn for
God, the greater will be your revelation of him."

Sri Ramakrishna was many-sided. Whenever he

talked about the intuitive knowledge of the God-head, he would talk as one who was a pure *jnani*, a knower of God. And whenever he talked about love and devotion, he talked as a pure lover and devotee of God. He impressed upon us very clearly that mere secular knowledge is nothing but vanity, and that one should struggle hard to attain spiritual knowledge, and love, and devotion to God alone.

Please tell us something about the Master's samadhi.

The Master used to experience many different kinds of samadhi. In some states his body would become stiff and motionless, like a log. It was easy for him to regain his normal consciousness from such a state, but at other times, when the samadhi was deeper, it would take him much longer to return to normal consciousness. At such times he would first draw a deep breath, like a drowning man coming up out of deep water. Then, for a while, he would reel and act like a drunken man; even his speech would be thick and incoherent. Gradually, however, he would regain his natural state.

Whenever you teach and give lectures, quote the teachings of Sri Ramakrishna. His words throw a clearer light on the scriptures and help to bring home the true import of their meaning.

Insincerity was the one thing Sri Ramakrishna could not stand. He loved those who loved God sincerely. He used to say: "If a man prays to God with a sincere heart, he is quickly freed from all impurities."

Most of the Master's nights were spent in samadhi or in chanting the Lord's name or in singing his praise. He seldom slept for more than an hour any night. Often I have seen him completely absorbed in samadhi for more than an hour at a time. Sometimes he would try to speak to us, but no words would come. Later he would say: "You see, I want to talk to you while I am in samadhi, but whenever I try to do so it seems as if the doors of my speech are locked." Many times as he was coming down to the normal plane he would be muttering, as though addressing his words to God whom he was still seeing.

He used to say, "To find God you must yearn for him," and he would tell this story: "An aspirant approached his teacher and asked to be shown the way to the attainment of God. The teacher took the disciple by the hand and led him to the river. There, without a word, he held the disciple's head under the water for some time. After a while he let go, and the disciple came up, choking and gasping for breath. He looked at his teacher in astonishment, and the teacher smiled at him and said: 'Well, how did it feel?' The disciple answered: 'I felt an intense longing for air!' 'Well,' said the teacher, 'when you can long for God with the same intensity as you longed for that breath of air you will surely attain him.' "

When Swami Vivekananda first came to Sri

Ramakrishna as a young man, he would often argue with him. At that time Swamiji believed only in the formless aspect of God and even told Sri Rama-krishna that he considered his visions of God as mere hallucinations of the brain. He would also scold the devotees when they went to bow down to the deities in the temple. This attitude annoyed many of the Master's disciples, but the Master himself was not disturbed. He could never be angry with Naren. He would say: "Naren is unique. There is none to equal him." Later on he gave Swamiji the vision of God in all his aspects, so that he too came to say: "Devote yourself to God—whether with form or without form —and you will reach him!"

Maharaj, many people are of the opinion that those who met Sri Ramakrishna did not need to struggle to find God. To know him was quite sufficient. Even the great devotee Ram Dutta held this view.

Ram Dutta was unique. He had true faith, a faith which grew in intensity and which lasted all his life. Few have such faith. With the majority it is merely lip faith.

Maharaj, many devotees who have seen the Holy Mother and have served holy men think it is not necessary for them to continue their spiritual struggles.

Merely to see the Holy Mother and to serve holy men is not enough. It is most necessary to practice renunciation and discrimination, and to live a contemplative life.

THE ONE PURPOSE of human life is to attain devotion to God and spiritual illumination; otherwise life is vain and meaningless. Eating, drinking, sleeping, and procreating are not the sole ends of human birth; these belong to the brutes. God is greatly manifest in the human body. Try to understand this truth.

Ah! Swamiji gave his heart's blood to build this monastery so that you young men might have the opportunity to devote your lives to God and practice spiritual disciplines. In fact, in his effort to make your life easier he over-exerted himself and shortened his own life. What intense love he had toward all mankind!

Sri Ramakrishna was revealed to the world at large through Swamiji. Know that their words and teachings are not different. Sri Ramakrishna was too great for the average mind to grasp; it was Swami Vivekananda who made his life and teachings understandable to all.

Study Swamiji's works carefully, for unless you understand his teachings it is useless to try to understand Sri Ramakrishna. Read and study the teachings of both, and at the same time devote yourself to the practice of japam and meditation. You are young now, and these are the best years of your life. Mold your minds now; when once the mind is molded there is nothing to fear. When you can bring the mind under control you will have achieved much. Whip it whenever it tries to run astray.

HOLD FAST to the lotus feet of the Lord. Remember him constantly; do not waste any more time in worldly thoughts. Struggle! Struggle hard to control the outgoing mind and fix it on God. When you can do this, you will realize what joy there is in spiritual life, what fun[1] it is! Ignorance must be overcome in this very life. This will not be easy unless you can devote yourself wholeheartedly to the work of the spirit. Faith is the one thing needed, intense faith! Let not doubts get hold of your mind.

But if doubts come, Maharaj?

Doubts will come until you have realized God; therefore you must hold fast to God and pray. Think to yourself: "God *is!* but because of the impurities of my mind I cannot see him. When my heart and mind have become purified, then, through his grace, I shall surely see him!"

God cannot be known by the finite mind. He is

[1]The word "fun" as applied to spiritual joy was characteristic of Swami Brahmananda, who wished by its use to do away with the chasm which exists in many minds between the high satisfactions of religion and the moods of simple happiness experienced in everyday life. Everyone likes fun: Why, then, should everyone not like God? For God, when all is said, is the real and only fun.

beyond the mind and far beyond the intellect. This apparent universe is a creation of the mind. The mind has conjured it up; it is its author, and the mind cannot go beyond its own domain.

Behind this mind of ours there is a subtle, spiritual mind, existing in seed-form. Through the practice of contemplation, prayer, and japam, this mind is developed, and with this development a new vision opens up and the aspirant realizes many spiritual truths. This, however, is not the final experience. The subtle mind leads the aspirant nearer to God, but it cannot reach God, the supreme Atman. Having reached this stage, the world no longer holds any charm for the aspirant; he becomes absorbed in the consciousness of God. This absorption leads to samadhi, an experience which cannot be described. It is beyond *is* and *is not.* There, there is neither happiness nor misery, neither light nor darkness. All is infinite Being—inexpressible.

Maharaj, how should we perform our worldly duties?

Do your duties conscientiously, and without attachment. Always remember that you are an instrument in the hands of God, and that God himself is the only doer. Keep your mind fixed in God. It is not always easy to keep the mind steady in God while working; the ego creeps in. But never be discouraged by your failures. Repeated failure is inevitable in the beginning, but keep your faith and redouble your efforts. Try hard to live up to your ideal.

Let your watchword be: "I must realize God in this very life!" After all, what is the use of this body and this mind if they do not help you to realize God? Do or die! What does it matter even if you die in the attempt!"

> *Maharaj, what is the significance of all these gods and goddesses? Do they really exist? And what is the meaning and purpose of ritualistic worship?*

The many gods and goddesses represent but so many different aspects of the one Godhead. Men differ in their temperaments and so are inclined to different ways of worship. To meet the needs of all, the scriptures prescribe four distinct methods of worship.

One method is the ritualistic worship of God embodied in an image or symbol. Higher than this is the worship of God with prayer and japam. By this means the aspirant prays and chants and meditates upon the shining form of his Chosen Ideal within his own heart.

Higher still is meditation. When a man practices this form of worship, he keeps up a constant flow of thought toward God and becomes absorbed in the living presence of his Chosen Ideal. He goes beyond prayer and japam, but the sense of duality remains.

The highest method of worship is meditation on the unity of the Atman and Brahman. This leads directly and immediately to God. The aspirant experiences Brahman; he knows that God *is*. It is an actual realization of the omnipresent Reality.

These are the different stages through which the aspirant progresses. It is of vital importance that a man begin his spiritual journey from where he is. If an average man is instructed to meditate on his union with the absolute Brahman, he will not understand. He will neither grasp the truth of it nor be able to follow the instructions. For a while he may try, but sooner or later he will tire of the struggle and give up.

However, if that same man is asked to worship God with flowers, incense, and other accessories of the ritualistic worship, his mind will gradually become concentrated on God and he will find joy in his worship. Through such worship, devotion to the performance of japam grows. The finer the mind becomes, the greater is its capacity for the higher forms of worship. Through japam the mind inclines toward meditation; thus the aspirant gradually and naturally moves toward his Ideal.

Take the illustration of a man standing in the courtyard of a house. He wants to reach the roof, but, instead of climbing the staircase step by step, he permits himself to be thrown up bodily. What happens? He is seriously hurt. So it is with the spiritual life. One should follow the gradual path, for, just as there are laws governing the physical world so are there laws governing the spiritual world also.

How may I check a distracting thought that persistently arises in my mind?

Think to yourself: "This thought is immensely harmful to me. It will be my ruin!" Impress the idea again and again upon your mind. The mind is extremely susceptible to suggestions and will learn whatever you teach it. Therefore, if through discrimination you can impress upon it the joy and fullness of the spiritual life and the folly of worldly attachments, it will devote itself more and more to God, and you will find yourself freed from all distracting thoughts.

The supreme ideal of the human life is to know God. Everyone must have this ideal firmly established in his life, and the ideal must never be lowered. He "who is smaller than the smallest, greater than the greatest" shines forth always and everywhere. He dwells within all beings, great and small; he dwells in the plants and herbs. He dwells everywhere in greater or lesser manifestation. Make that one supreme, all-pervading Spirit your ideal. Even after a little effort to realize him you will see what fun it is! You will find in him an inexhaustible fountain of joy. You have seen enough of one side of life—now see the other side, the real side. "Knock and it shall be opened unto you." A veil is hiding the Reality. Remove that veil and you will find him. If you will apply yourself to the attainment of this ideal, the whole world will be transformed for you.

Maharaj, what rules of diet should one follow?

That is a difficult question to answer. Men differ so widely in their constitutions that it is hardly possible to lay down any hard and fast rule about food. One kind of food may be agreeable to your constitution, and yet may do me harm. For this reason the scriptures do not specifically advise any diet but only warn against rich foods.

Should we avoid eating meat, since it entails killing?

Nonsense! The Buddhists say: "Harmlessness is the highest virtue." What does this mean? You can understand the significance of this only when you have attained samadhi, when you have reached enlightenment and have seen God in all creatures. Until then mere talk is useless. When you can see the same God in the ant as in yourself, then you can practice this virtue. You may talk of not killing, but can you possibly avoid killing? What would you eat? Potatoes? Plant a potato underground, it shoots forth young sprouts. Has the potato no life? Would you eat rice? Plant the paddy grain in the earth, it grows into a rice plant. You want to drink water? Examine a drop of water under a microscope and see how many millions of tiny lives are there. You must breathe to live. Yet with every breath you kill millions of creatures. Do you see any harm in that? You think you lose your religion if you take a little fish. Such arguments are foolish. The ancient Hindus held no such ideas. These are later Buddhist and Vaishnavite interpolations.

SAMADHI IS GENERALLY CLASSIFIED as of two kinds. In the first, the *savikalpa samadhi*, one experiences the mystic vision of the spiritual form of God, while the consciousness of individuality remains. In the second, the *nirvikalpa samadhi*, a man loses his individuality and goes beyond the vision of the form of God. The whole universe disappears. Besides these two there is yet another kind of samadhi called *ananda* (blissful) samadhi. If an ordinary man attains this experience, his body and brain cannot stand the intense ecstatic joy; he cannot live more than twenty-one days.

Between the eyebrows there is a third eye, the eye of wisdom. When this eye is opened a fountain of joy is released, and the whole universe seems merged in bliss.

One day, in the course of his teaching, Sri Ramakrishna spoke about the manifestation of Brahman as sound—the Logos. Later, when I sat for meditation I took this as my subject, and it was not long before the sound Brahman was revealed to me.

Sri Ramakrishna one day told me: "Once, while I was meditating in the temple, screen after screen of maya was removed from my consciousness, and I saw a light more brilliant than a million suns. From that light there came forth a spiritual form which again melted away into the formless."

The body is the temple of God, and one should practice worship and meditation within it. When the consciousness merges into the *sahasrara*, the mind does not feel inclined to come back. There you realize that what is outside is also within yourself.

Though temples may serve as aids to the beginner, they are but symbols of God's greatest of all temples, the human heart.

WITHIN THE PALACE of seven gates there dwells a king with whom a poor man begs an audience. The king's minister grants his request and leads him through the gates to the royal presence. At each gate there stands a richly dressed officer, and each time the poor man asks the minister if that is the king. The minister answers, "No," each time, until they have passed the seventh gate and the king stands before them in all his splendor and beauty. Then no question is asked; the man recognizes his king. So it is with the guru. Like the king's minister, he leads the disciple through the different stages of spiritual unfoldment, until he leaves him with the Lord.

But know this! There is no greater guru than your own mind. When the mind has been purified by prayer and contemplation it will direct you from within. Even in your daily duties, this inner guru will guide you and will continue to help you until the goal is reached. Have intense love for God and the mind will remain always tranquil and pure.

The easiest way to purify and steady the mind is to retire into solitude, control all cravings, and engage yourself in contemplation and meditation. The more you occupy the mind with holy thoughts, the greater will be your spiritual unfoldment. Just as a cow yields much milk when it is well fed, so when the mind is fed spiritual food it will yield greater tranquillity. Spiritual food consists of meditation, prayer, contemplation, and japam.

Another way to steady the mind is to let it wander, but to keep a steady watch over its wanderings. After a while the mind itself becomes tired and comes back to find peace in God. If you watch your mind, your mind will in turn watch over you.

It is good to rise early in the morning. The time best suited for contemplation is when night passes into day, and when day passes into night. It is then that the *sushumna* becomes active, and one breathes through both nostrils. As a general rule, we breathe through only one nostril at a time. This causes restlessness of the mind. Spiritual aspirants should observe when they are breathing through both nostrils; the sushumna is active then. Those times are the most helpful to contemplation, and we should take advantage of them.

Free your mind from cravings and attachments. Practice spiritual disciplines, and your mind will become pure and steady. If a man does not struggle hard to realize God, he remains steeped in ignorance. Therefore struggle, struggle, and God will be revealed. Accept all trials and tribulations boldly. Welcome them, for through them you shall surely find peace.

The easiest method of realization is to remember God constantly. Even as a man welcomes his friend, and entertains him with food, drink, and conversation, so must you entertain God in your thoughts. Converse freely with him. Know him as your very own, and you will find peace in him.

Who can fathom the mystery of God? He is infinite and formless, and yet he is also with form. He incarnates himself as man. Verily, it is beyond the power of the mind to understand the devious ways through which God leads man to himself. Sometimes the path is smooth, sometimes it is thorny, and sometimes it is like an impassable mountain, but still he leads man safely to himself, if he will only take refuge in him.

It is maya which prevents the mind and senses from desiring to experience God, but a man who has realized him has risen above all the charms and attractions of maya. Maya reveals her mysteries only to him who has gone beyond maya.

Being chained to maya, man does not realize how great is his suffering as he whirls around on the wheel of birth and death. The body decays day by day while man still sleeps in maya, forgetting the sacred mission for which he was born. The one unique advantage of this human birth over all other forms of life is that it is by man alone that God can be realized. Therefore, forget the body and its comforts; shake off the delusion of birth and death. Shake off the illusory peace of maya and find the real peace—the everlasting peace of God.

SRI RAMAKRISHNA USED TO SAY that a man will surely attain God if he possesses in an intense degree three kinds of love—the love a chaste wife feels toward her husband, the attraction the worldly man feels toward the world, and the attachment the miser feels toward his hoarded wealth. This means that the mind must be one-pointed and completely free of all desires but the desire to know and love God. Sri Krishna says in the Gita:

> Lay down all duties
> In me, your refuge.
> Fear no longer,
> For I will save you
> From sin and from bondage.

Surrender yourself wholeheartedly to God. Take refuge in him. Pray constantly with a pure, sincere heart: "O Lord, I do not know what is good and what is bad for me. I am entirely dependent on you. Grant me what I most need for the spiritual life. Take me along the path which will lead me to the greatest good. Give me the faith and strength constantly to remember you and meditate on you."

It is no easy thing to dedicate oneself heart and soul to the Lord. Many people boast: "I have surrendered myself and my all to God. I do only what he tells me to do." But if we observe their lives we see differently. For the good they do they claim the credit and they boast of their achievements; but when adversity or trouble overtakes them they cry out against the Lord and blame him for their misfortunes.

We judge men by their actions, but God looks into their innermost minds. Be sure of this: God runs to him who prays with a sincere heart. Be pure in heart and always make your thoughts and lips one.

Only one in a million sincerely longs for God, and few sustain that longing. Therefore you must try to intensify that longing. Whatever you do, whether you are sitting, or lying down, or eating, or working, pray constantly: "O Lord, make me able to understand and receive that grace which I know you are ready to give me." Know that your time on earth is but short, and that your real home is at the lotus feet of the Lord.

In his folly man will deny the very existence of God because of his own lack of comprehension. He prefers to rely upon his own intellect, little realizing how unstable that intellect is. Even though what he accepts as true today he rejects as false tomorrow, yet he thinks that what appears as true to himself today is the final truth and must be accepted by all.

The Lord alone knows all the subtle ways by which a man may be deluded.

One who has known God does not limit him. To him, God is not a matter of opinion: God *is*. He is boundless love and infinite mercy. He is beyond the grasp of the intellect. He who has realized God understands his mysteries. For him there is nothing hidden. The gates of knowledge are open, and he knows that he belongs to God even as God belongs to him.

Intelligence is but another name for ignorance, because its area is limited. Therefore, if a man wants to attain all knowledge and understand all mysteries, let him devote himself to the knowledge of God.

As children swing around a pillar in their play, holding tightly to it for their support, so must you hold fast to God—the Pillar of life. Whichever path you follow, whether it be the path of work, or of devotion, or of knowledge, you will reach him. Hold fast to the Pillar, and your life will be blessed, and you in turn will become a blessing to mankind.

Maharaj, is initiation really necessary?

Yes! Initiation is very important. With the aid of a mantram it is easier to practice concentration of the mind on one Chosen Ideal of God. Without the mantram the mind wanders from one conception of God to another, and never succeeds in concentrating upon any. And without achieving perfect concentration nothing can be accomplished in the spiritual life. Therefore the aid of a guru is very necessary. He helps the disciple to choose his own particular Ideal, according to his temperament, and then gives the mantram best suited to the attainment of concentration on that Ideal.

With unwavering faith in the words of the guru, the disciple must regularly practice repetition of the mantram and meditation on its meaning. Thus will he find peace of heart.

The path of spirituality is hard to follow. No matter how clever or how intelligent a man may be, without the aid of an illumined guide he is sure to stumble on the way.

Maharaj, I have been practicing spiritual disciplines, but as yet I have acquired no taste for them. What shall I do?

The taste for spiritual life cannot be had all at once. No! One has to struggle hard for it. All our energies must be concentrated toward that one achievement; they must not be wasted in any other direction. Onward, onward! Never be satisfied with your present state of growth. Try to create a burning dissatisfaction within yourself. Ask yourself, "What progress am I making? None!" and apply yourself ever more diligently to the task. Sri Ramakrishna used to cry out at the close of each day: "O Mother, another day has gone, and I have not seen you!"

Every night before you go to sleep, think for a while how much time you have spent in doing good deeds and how much time you have wasted; how much time you have spent in meditation and how much you have wasted in idleness. Make your mind strong through the observance of continence and the practice of meditation.

You cannot buy God. His vision comes only through his grace. Does this mean that you should not practice spiritual disciplines? Certainly you must practice, otherwise passions will create havoc in you.

A rich man employs a porter whose duty it is to see that neither thieves, nor cows, nor sheep, nor any other intruder enter the compound. Man's mind is his porter, and the stronger the mind becomes, the better. The mind has also been likened to a restive horse. Such a horse may carry its rider along the wrong path, and only he who can hold the reins and check the horse can keep to the right path.

Struggle on! Do you think that everything is achieved merely by wearing the gerua cloth, or by the renunciation of hearth and home? What spiritual experiences have you had? Time is flying. Waste no more time, for at most you have only another three or four years in which to struggle intensively. After that your body and mind will grow weak and infirm and your efforts will be limited. What can be achieved without diligence?

You may think: "Let us have yearning, faith, and devotion first, then we shall begin our spiritual practices." But is that possible? Can we see the day before the break of dawn? When the Lord comes, love, devotion, and faith follow him as his retinue.

Nothing can be achieved without spiritual discipline. Have you not seen what severe disciplines even the *avatars* underwent? Has anything been gained without labor? What tremendous austerities were practiced by Buddha, Shankara, and others! What burning renunciation!

Real faith cannot be had at the beginning. First realization, then faith. At first the spiritual aspirant must pin his faith—blind faith, it may be—in the words of his guru or some great soul; only then can he advance toward the goal.

Do you know Sri Ramakrishna's parable of the oyster? The oyster floats about on the surface of the water with its shell wide open, waiting for a little drop of the Swati-rain (the rain which falls when the star Swati or Arcturus is in the ascendant). As soon as it gets the raindrop it dives down to the bottom of the sea and there forms a fine pearl. You, like the oyster, have received the raindrop; you have the grace of your guru; now dive deep into the ocean of bliss and form the pearl—let God be revealed.

Be self-reliant. Self-effort is absolutely necessary to success in the spiritual life. Follow some spiritual discipline for at least three years, and then, if you find you have made no tangible progress, you may come back and slap my face!

Japam and meditation are impossible unless you

can transcend *rajas* and *tamas* and become established in *sattwa*. Before you can reach that transcendental plane from which there is no return you must transcend sattwa also.

How blessed is this human birth! Man alone can find God. To realize him must be man's only purpose. Strive hard to reach him and be free in this very life.

The mind is to be raised, step by step, from the gross state to the subtle, then to the causal state, then higher still, to the Great Cause (Mahakarana) and finally to samadhi. Resign yourself utterly to the Lord. He is everything. There is nothing besides. "Verily all this is Brahman." Everything is his and his alone.

Never be calculating. Is self-surrender possible in a day? When that is achieved everything is achieved. One must struggle hard for it. Existence is eternal. The span of man's life is at most a hundred years. Give up the pleasures of these hundred years if you want to enjoy eternal life and, with it, eternal bliss.

IN THE BEGINNING of spiritual life it is very good to plan a definite routine. A certain length of time should be given to the practices of meditation, japam, and study. Whether you like it or not, follow your routine regularly. By so doing, you will gradually create a permanent habit. Perhaps now you do not enjoy meditating, but as you form the habit you will come to the point where you will actually feel unhappy if you do not meditate. When you reach this stage, you will know that you have advanced along the spiritual path.

When a man is hungry or cannot sleep at night, he is restless and unhappy. When you can feel this same restlessness and unhappiness because you have not seen God, then know that God is very near.

Reach the Immortal and find immortality. Then it will not matter where you are or what you are doing. Turn the iron into gold by the touch of the philosopher's stone, then, whether you bury it or keep it in a neat box, it will not matter. It will always remain gold.

Sri Ramakrishna used to say: "Realize that you are one with Brahman, then do as you please." By this he meant, first attain love and knowledge, realize God, then it does not matter how you live or what you do. One who has reached this state, however, can never take a false step.

Many are the obstacles to a godly life. Therefore it is necessary to pray earnestly to the Lord to remove these obstacles. Yearn for his grace.

Many are the worldly impressions already accumulated in your mind, and many are the impressions created in this life also. As you struggle against them, they will seem to grow stronger, so that he alone truly conquers them who never loses sight of the ideal and never gives up the struggle.

Within each one of us there are two currents flowing. One carries us toward God and the other carries us toward the world. One current takes you along the path of renunciation to God; the other tries to pull you toward worldly enjoyments. We must choose between them. As a result of this choice we become either gods or brutes.

The tempting objects of the world lie before man's eyes in all their glittering and delusive splendor, so that he feels no need even to consider the probability of anything higher or grander. He may hear about the higher ideal of life, but he rationalizes by asking himself what guarantee there is that God can be known, or that a greater joy can be reached. He sees no reason why he should give up today's pleasure for tomorrow's promise. Thinking thus, he jumps farther into the fire, until, burned and frustrated, he realizes his folly. Then he longs for peace, but often the longing comes too late. So enslaved has his mind become, that, even though he may earnestly desire to change his ways, he is helpless to do so in this life.

Maharaj, you spoke of the practices of puja, meditation, continence, and study of the scriptures. What do you mean by puja?

Puja means both external ritualistic worship and mental worship. In ritualistic worship certain accessories are necessary. These are sometimes difficult to procure; therefore, the mental worship is more convenient for you. First worship the Chosen Ideal mentally with flowers, incense, etc., and then practice meditation and mental japam. In purely mental japam the mantram is repeated without moving the lips, but in ordinary japam the mantram is repeated silently with the movement of the lips.

As you meditate on your Chosen Ideal, think of him as bright and effulgent, and that everything shines because of his light. Think of him as living and conscious. As you continue thus, the form of your Chosen Ideal will gradually melt into the formless, into the Infinite. Then will follow a vivid sense of the Living Presence, until, finally, the eye of wisdom will open and the Infinite will be directly perceived. Ah! that is another realm, far beyond this universe! After this experience the universe appears as nothing; the mind is dissolved and you experience savikalpa samadhi. This leads gradually to the realization of the nirvikalpa samadhi—absolute union with God. This experience is beyond all thought and speech; there is nothing to be seen, nothing to be heard. All is infinite silence! It is "beyond duality and nonduality." There are some who, having reached this state, look upon the body as an obstacle in the way of an unbroken spiritual experience, and cast it off, even while in samadhi. It is like breaking an earthen vessel.

Sri Ramakrishna used to give the following illustration to explain this highest state of spiritual realization; imagine several vessels filled with water, with the sun reflected in each one. Break each vessel until only one remains, with the sun fully reflected in that one. Finally you break even the last of the vessels, and what remains? The sun itself. Similarly, the self-luminous Brahman is reflected in the vessels of mind, senses, ego, etc. Break these vessels, one after another, and go beyond the physical consciousness, the subtle body, and the causal body, until you reach savikalpa samadhi, when you will see God. But here, even in this stage, the sense of separateness still remains, the last vessel is still to be broken. Break it, and what remains? Brahman and Brahman alone. Who is there left to see whom? Who to describe whom?

Maharaj, some think of the Chosen Ideal as the all-pervading spirit. Is this also a form of meditation?

Yes, certainly. Everyone should practice this meditation, but not at the beginning. This should be done only after some progress in spiritual life has been made. The presence of God must be realized everywhere. He who is personal and has form is also impersonal and without form. He dwells in all beings. He pervades land and water, hills and valleys, sky and stars—he pervades all things.

The scriptures speak of service to the guru as a necessary means to spiritual realization. How far is this true?

Service to the guru is necessary at the preliminary stage, but later the mind itself plays the part of the guru. The guru must not be looked upon as an ordinary human being. His physical body is the temple of God; if one can serve the guru with this idea always in mind, one acquires an intense love for him, which later develops into an intense love for God.

Meditate upon the guru in the *sahasrara*, and then merge the form into that of the Chosen Ideal. Sri Ramakrishna said very explicitly: "At the time of meditation the guru appears before the disciple in vision; he points to the disciple's Chosen Ideal and says, 'Look, there is your Chosen Ideal.' Then he himself merges into the form of the Chosen Ideal." Thus there is really no difference between the guru and God.

There are so many divine experiences. How can I tell you of them all? Follow the spiritual path earnestly and sincerely. Through religious practices the mind will become pure, and you will understand many truths. There is no limit to them. Lose yourself in God. Try to meditate within the shrine of your own heart. What that shrine is will be revealed to you as you continue the practice.

If the aspirant finds even a little joy in meditation, he is at once encouraged to proceed; isn't that so, Maharaj?

True. But in the higher spiritual state there is neither joy nor sorrow, pain nor pleasure, existence nor non-existence. The joy that you speak of is only a help during the period of spiritual practices. The boat needs a favorable wind to reach its destination. But when it once arrives, it no longer matters whether the wind is favorable or not. Joy is like that favorable wind; it helps the aspirant along the spiritual path.

Knowledge, the knower, and the object known—these three lose themselves in the Absolute; that is all the scriptures can tell us. What takes place after this, no one is able to describe. It is directly experienced only by one who practices meditation. Only God can know himself. Be a god, that you may know the infinite God. In that knowledge there is neither want nor fear. The very thought of such knowledge is uplifting.

To live in God is pure joy. Some enlightened souls experience the one undivided Existence. Then they know that the seeming multiplicity of the universe is God's divine play. They know that the infinite God is born as an avatar for his own divine sport. Once when Sri Krishna was dancing in ecstasy, one shepherdess said to another, "Look, my friend, the Truth of Vedanta is dancing!" Sri Krishna is the supreme Brahman. He is the infinite, changeless Spirit playing as man. Beyond this there is yet another deeper and fathomless spiritual experience.

Maharaj: Well, how are you getting along with your spiritual practices?

Not very well, Maharaj. I am very unhappy; my mind is so restless. I must have been born with

*some very evil tendencies which are now standing
in the way of my spiritual practices.*

My boy, you must not talk like that. Try to practice
japam at dead of night; if that is not possible, do it
during the early hours of the morning. Perform *purascharan.* Waste no more of your valuable time. Lose
yourself in prayer and meditation; otherwise, how
can the door to spiritual truth be opened?

The spiritual aspirant should eat very little food
after sunset. Begin by taking three-fourths of your
usual amount, then reduce the quantity to one half.
In the beginning you may notice it, but the body will
soon adjust itself and remain healthy and active.

(Maharaj then referred to the days when he practiced spiritual disciplines in the company of his brother-disciples, when they took only one meal during the
twenty-four hours.)

The aspirant should first learn about the spiritual
path from some great soul and then follow it methodically. If he proceeds haphazardly he cannot make
much progress, and if he gives up entirely, the effort
to begin again will be twice as difficult. But no effort
is wasted. Lust, greed, anger, all gradually leave a
man who practices spiritual disciplines.

Your mind at present is covered over by rajas and
tamas. It must be made pure and subtle and raised to
the state of sattwa, then you will find joy in your
practices, and will want to devote more and more
time to them. Later, when the mind has attained

perfect purity, you will have but one desire—to devote yourself to contemplation always. Because the mind is gross it runs after gross things, but as it becomes pure and subtle it will run after God—the pure consciousness. When the mind grows subtle, its power increases and the aspirant is immediately able to grasp the truth of God.

When you sit for meditation first think of a divine, blissful form. This will bring a soothing effect upon your nerves; otherwise meditation will be dry and tedious. Think of the form of your Chosen Ideal, smiling and full of bliss.

Be up and doing! Waste no more time. The senses now are strong, and must be kept under control. This is a difficult task, no doubt, but if you practice meditation continuously for seven or eight years you will find peace and bliss, and enjoy the fruits of your practices. Even after one year of steady practice you will find some result. Many women disciples are making rapid progress. Should not you also strive for that? Women generally have greater results in less time because their faith is greater.

Believe me, the Lord is always with you. Practice even a little, and he will extend his hand to help you. He will protect you from all miseries and unhappiness. How unbounded is his grace! How can I make you understand?

So far you have merely heard about these spiritual truths. Now realize them. You have done enough studying and reasoning, now do some spiritual exer-

cises. Choose that aspect of God which most appeals
to you, and when you feel a growing devotion toward
that one aspect, when you feel a steadfast love toward
your Chosen Ideal, you will love God in all his aspects.

While practicing japam one should meditate on the
form of the Chosen Ideal, otherwise it is not effective.
If you cannot think of the whole form, think of a part.
Begin by meditating on the lotus feet of the Lord.
Even if you fail many times, try again. Success is
certain. Practice will make all things easy.

Is meditation an easy thing? Remember, it is next
only to samadhi. Try to leave everything to the Lord.
Resign yourself entirely to him. Devotion, self-surrender, and all other virtues will grow from within as
you practice meditation.

Maharaj, how can the kundalini *be awakened?*

According to some there are special exercises by
which the kundalini can be awakened, but I believe
it can best be awakened by the practice of japam and
meditation. The practice of japam is specially suited
to this present age; and there is no spiritual practice
easier than this, but meditation must accompany the
repetition of the mantram.

*Does meditation mean thinking of the form of
the Deity?*

Meditation means thinking of the Divine both with form and without form.

Maharaj, does the guru decide whether one should meditate on God with form or without form?

Yes, he does. But in time the mind itself becomes the guru. Sometimes the mind is inclined to think of God with form, and again, at another time it prefers to think of the formless aspect. The human guru is not always available, but as the aspirant goes on with his spiritual practices his power of comprehension increases, so that his mind is able to act as his guide.

The mind is bound down by its attachment to the body, the senses, and the objects of sense. Thus its energies run out through various channels and are wasted. Snap the bonds of attachment! Collect the scattered forces of the mind and direct them toward the one Reality. This is the great task of the spiritual aspirant.

Concentrate the whole mind and direct it toward God until he becomes revealed. Now is the time for spiritual practices. You are young now. When you grow older the mind loses its vigor. Therefore be up and doing! Begin your spiritual life this moment; direct your mind toward God either through japam, or through meditation, or through discrimination.

Know that each of these means is equally effective. Take any one of them and drown yourself in the ocean of bliss. Ask no more questions. First do something, and then ask questions!

Maharaj, is the kundalini awakened by the grace of the guru?

Through the grace of the guru everything can be had, even the knowledge of Brahman, but this grace is not easily obtained. You must work hard for it. Begin now. Devote yourself to spiritual disciplines; plunge into the very depth of your soul. To do this it is advisable to establish a definite routine for the practice of japam and meditation, and to follow it with unwavering tenacity, whether you like it or not.

Maharaj: How are you progressing with your spiritual practices?

Not very well, Maharaj! I find so little time for them. There is so much work to be done.

Nonsense! It is a mistake to think that you cannot meditate for lack of time. The real cause is restlessness of mind.

Work and worship must go hand in hand. It is a very good thing if one can devote oneself entirely to spiritual practices, but how many can do that? There are two types of men who can sit still without working. One is the idiot, who is too dull to be active, and the other is the saint who has gone beyond all activity. As the Gita says: "Freedom from activity is never achieved by abstaining from action."

> Let him who would climb
> In meditation
> To heights of the highest
> Union with Brahman
> Take for his path
> The yoga of action:
> Then when he nears
> That height of oneness
> His acts will fall from him,
> His path will be tranquil.

Work, therefore, is a means to reach the stage of meditation. Even those who give up work and lead an ascetic life have to devote some time to the necessary requirements of living. None can live without work. As Sri Krishna says, "Your very nature will force you to work."

Learn to work for the Lord instead of working for yourself. Know that you are worshiping the Lord through your work. If you can work with this attitude, work will not bind you; on the contrary, it will improve you in every way, physically, mentally, intellectually, morally, and spiritually. Offer yourself, body and soul, to the Lord. Give yourself entirely to him. Say to him: "I give myself, body and soul, to you, O Lord. Do with me what you will. I am your servant, ready to serve you to the best of my ability."

If you can really do this, the responsibility for your spiritual well-being rests with him. But this resignation should be inspired by the right spirit and complete faith. No doubt must enter your heart; it is no use "taking the name of God to cross the river and at the same time raising your cloth to keep it dry."[1]

For five or six years, after the passing away of our Master, we led a wandering life. Then, one day Swamiji (Swami Vivekananda) called me aside and said: "There is nothing in this wandering life. Work for the sake of the Lord." We worked hard in those days, but it did us no harm; rather, it did us good. We had great faith in Swamiji's words. I tell you, you must have infinite faith in these two great souls, Sri Ramakrishna and Swamiji, and work for them.

[1]This reference is to Sri Ramakrishna's parable of the milkmaid and the brahmin priest. A milkmaid used to supply milk to a brahmin priest on the other side of the river. Owing to the irregularities of the boat service, the woman was sometimes late. One day the priest rebuked her for the delay, and she explained that sometimes she had to wait a long time for the boatman to ferry her across. The priest said: "But, my good woman! people cross the ocean of life by uttering the name of God. Cannot you cross even this little river?" From that day forward she was never late with the milk. One day the priest asked her why it was that she was never late any more, and she said simply: "I take the name of God and cross the river just as you told me!" The priest was astonished, and wanted to see for himself, so he went to the river with the woman, and watched her as she uttered the name of God and started to walk across the water. Halfway across, the woman turned and saw the priest following her, timidly holding his skirt up out of the water, and she said: "Why is it, Sir, that you are repeating the name of the Lord and at the same time holding up your skirt to keep it dry. Have you no faith?"

Work and worship must be harmonized. This at first may seem difficult, but one must try again and again. Sri Ramakrishna used to say: "The new-born calf tries to stand up, but it falls down many times. Still it never gives up; finally, after repeated efforts, it is not only able to stand, but it learns to run also."

It is excellent training for the mind to take up some form of work at the beginning of the spiritual life. When the mind is trained it can be applied to meditation and other spiritual practices. The mind that is allowed to drift at one time will drift at the time of meditation also.

There comes a time when the spiritually advanced man wants to devote himself solely to meditation and prayer. When that time comes, work drops away from him of itself. However, this happens only when the mind is spiritually awakened. If one who is not thus awakened should attempt to lead a life of exclusive spiritual practice by sheer effort of the will, it can last only for a few days; then comes monotony, sometimes followed by madness. Again there are others, who follow the spiritual path in a haphazard way and at the same time keep their minds busy with worldly things. That is not good.

Great strength can be acquired through the practice of continence. A true celibate can do the work of twenty-five men. Practice continence, japam, and meditation, and seek the company of the holy.

Not all men know what is best for them; therefore they should seek the society of holy men. Unless a man spends some time in solitude or in the company of the holy, he cannot understand his own mind. It is very difficult to grow spiritually in the midst of tumult and confusion.

I give freedom to all. I want everyone to advance along his own way, but when I find a devotee who is unable to do this, I come to his aid.

Life, eternal life, is before you! What matters it, if you devote a few lives to the service of God, even supposing they are spent in vain? But I tell you, this cannot be. You will see for yourself to what great spiritual heights you will soar through the grace of Sri Ramakrishna.

Give up this easy-going life, otherwise it will be impossible for you to perform your spiritual practices properly. No matter what work you do, do it with your whole heart. That is the secret of work, as Swamiji used to say.

Set yourself to work for the Lord, and before you begin any task remember the Lord and offer your salutations to him. Do this from time to time while you are working, and also when you have finished. Spend all your time thinking of the life, teachings, and commandments of Sri Ramakrishna. Know in your heart that the work you are doing you are doing for him.

Strive to attain tranquillity. Do not give way to inertia, but struggle to gain spiritual calmness. If you allow your mind to wander and lead a purposeless life, a bad reaction is bound to follow. Passions will overcome you. Through the practice of japam and meditation the senses are controlled of themselves. But in the beginning they must be kept in check.

Practice japam and meditation. Gradually after continued practice you will enjoy sitting for long periods of time absorbed in God. The beginner, however, should start with short periods at a time, four or five times a day. Practice japam, whether you like it or not. As you persist, the mind is certain to become absorbed in contemplation. To attain spiritual tranquillity you must keep up a regular practice, even against your inclinations. Spiritual awakening is bound to come, and when it does, all the passions that ever existed in you will be forgotten.

WHY DO I INSIST that you devote yourselves heart and soul to the Lord? When we were your age, Sri Ramakrishna kept careful watch over our spiritual practices. In youth the mind is like unbaked clay, and can be molded into any shape. Your minds are still young and pure; they have not been baked in the fire of worldliness; therefore, they can be easily directed toward God. If the mind is molded now, you will achieve your purpose; you will not be troubled by distractions.

The mind is like a package of mustard seeds. If the seeds are once scattered, it is difficult to gather them up again. Likewise, when the energies of the mind have been scattered, as one grows older it is very difficult to collect them and turn the mind toward God.

Make God the be-all and end-all of your life. Devote yourself sincerely to realizing him, and you will be free from all sorrow and pain. You will inherit eternal happiness.

Man seeks happiness in the world, but does he find it? In his mad pursuit he toils hard and runs hither and thither after many objects, only to find shadows after all. His life ebbs; he dies in vain. Leave these fleeting pleasures of the world behind you; give your mind to God, be devoted to him, and you will find real happiness. Devote your mind to the world and to the pleasures of the world, and great will be your suffering; devote your mind to God, and great will be your joy. No matter what riches you may possess, no matter what prospects you may have for living a happy and prosperous life, you still will not find lasting happiness. Pain follows pleasure, and every action brings its own reaction. Nothing lasts, but the one true happiness which is to be found in God.

You are boys—young boys. Your minds have not yet received any worldly impressions. If you can struggle now, you will be able to escape life's sorrows and miseries.

Never forget the ideal of human life. We have not inherited this human birth to waste it in eating, drinking, and sleeping like animals. Since you have been born as a human being, spurn all worldly enjoyments and resolve to realize God. Never waver in your purpose, even if it means to die in the attempt. Enjoy the ecstasy of devotion and spiritual practice now, and then enter the doors of infinite bliss forever.

The most important aim in spiritual life is the attainment of God's grace. The breeze of grace is always blowing; unfurl your sails. Give up worldly enjoyments and completely resign yourself to the Lord. You cannot love God and the world at the same time. If you want God, shun temporal pleasures. Ask yourself: "What is it I want? Do I want this fleeting life of transient pleasures, or do I want the eternal bliss of everlasting life?"

When a man has renounced all worldly cravings and regards God as his own, God is very near. Such a man binds God to him with the fetters of love.

Think of him as your very own. Pray to him, "Lord, reveal yourself to me!" God cannot remain unmoved by the pleas of such a devotee. He hastens to him and takes him in his arms. Oh, how inexpressible is that joy! How boundless that bliss! Only he can know who has had that experience, compared to which all worldly pleasures seem insipid and worthless.

Sri Ramakrishna used to say: "He who has given up sense-enjoyments for God's sake has already covered three parts of the journey." Is it easy to renounce bodily cravings? Only if one has God's grace and has practiced severe spiritual disciplines in past lives, can he have the strength to renounce the world in this life. Purify your mind so that no worldly desire can arise in it.

You have renounced everything and pledged your

life to God. But remember, it is very difficult to lead a pure and unsullied life. You may think it is easy, but let me tell you, it is like walking on the sharp edge of a razor.

Perfect continence is the sole condition of success in spiritual life, but it is difficult, even impossible, to practice absolute purity without love and faith in God. The world is full of temptations which arouse passions; every day you will see ninety-nine percent of the people rushing in mad pursuit after sensual pleasures. Your mind is in constant danger of becoming contaminated; therefore, you must engage your mind in thinking good thoughts, studying good books, and discussing uplifting subjects. You must spend your time in worship of God, in service to holy men, and in contemplation. This is the only way to mold your character.

First of all, be firm in your vow of chastity. Everything else will follow. You cannot live a continent life unless you devote yourself to God, and without continence realization of God is impossible. Unless you realize God you will not find happiness, and without happiness life is vain. Therefore I beg you, my dear children, struggle, make an effort, and soon you will find faith and devotion awakening within you. You will be blessed by the vision of God, and you will become the heirs of immortal bliss.

Maharaj, we have all come here to the monastery with the same ideal and purpose, renouncing

*our own hearth and home. Why is it then that we
cannot live in harmony with one another?*

My child, you must all learn to bear and forbear.
Sri Ramakrishna used to say, "He who forbears,
lives!" Even people living in the world have to bear
many things. The greatest strength of character is to
live in harmony with all. No one can find peace if he
hurts another. Never utter one word that would hurt
another. "Tell the truth, but never tell a harsh truth."

Look at the many different kinds of people who
come to me; some are good, some are bad, but I love
them all equally. If I should drive away the weak and
the depraved, where would they find refuge? If I pick
the wool from a blanket, nothing will be left. It is easy
to live in harmony with saints, but real strength lies
in living in harmony with all beings.

A YOUNG DISCIPLE decided that he would like to go
away to some solitary place to practice austerities.
With this intention he presented himself before
Maharaj and asked his permission. When Maharaj
heard of the boy's intention, he became very anxious
and said: "Go and ask Swami Shivananda to come
here." The Swami came and seated himself beside
Maharaj. Anxiously Maharaj said: "Look, brother,
this boy wants to go away from here to practice austerities. I cannot understand why our boys' minds
work in this way. This place has been made holy by

the exemplary life of the late Swami Ramakrishnananda. What a wonderful atmosphere he has
created in this monastery. Where else could such a
holy atmosphere be found? Why do they have to
practice austerities? Have we not done all that for
them? The trouble is, they do not know their own
minds."

Turning to the disciple, Maharaj continued: "As
long as you think 'God is *there,*' you will find no
peace. When you know and can feel that he is *here,
here* (pointing to his heart), you will find peace."

WHAT IS THE USE of wandering about from place to
place? Have you not seen hundreds of such wandering monks? And what have they achieved? Are you
to become like them? Swamiji did not want you boys
to be like these wandering monks. He founded this
monastery toward one great end: and that is to realize
God. Consider that, and try to live your life and mold
your character accordingly. The spiritual practices of
one single man are enough to make a monastery vibrate with holiness.

Oh, what a wonderful spiritual atmosphere there
was at the Dakshineswar temple when Sri Ramakrishna was living there! The moment our boat
touched the steps of the landing stage we felt as if we
had reached heaven itself! And what a wonderful
love existed between us brother-disciples. Between
you, there is no such sweet relationship. A holy man
should be sweet in temperament, and should never
speak harshly to anyone. Ah! I remember a holy man

I once met at Brindaban. He was a regular visitor at the temple. For a few days he did not come, and I missed him. When he came again I asked him the reason for his absence. He explained that he had had a sore foot. One day in the crowd the foot of another devotee had touched his and temporarily disabled him. I was deeply touched by the way that holy man explained the incident. He did not complain that he had been trampled upon by some careless person. To him every foot was the Lord's foot, and the Lord had placed his foot upon him!

If only you could all be sweet and have love in your hearts, then there would be great harmony. You have to make the Lord the center of all your affections.

In this monastery you have so many opportunities to do Swamiji's work; you cannot always meditate.

You are young; this is the time to practice spiritual disciplines. What can you do when you are old? Develop love in your heart and you will achieve everything. You have become dry! Where is your early enthusiasm? You seem to be quite satisfied with your present condition, but I tell you, do not remain satisfied with yourself as you are now. Contentment with the external conditions, yes, but never be contented with your state of spiritual growth. Become dissatisfied. Try to move ever onward in your search. Do not stop until you have found the diamond mine![1]

[1]Referring to a parable of Sri Ramakrishna. A woodcutter, going into the forest to gather wood, met a monk who said: "Go deeper into the wood." The woodcutter did as he was told and soon came to a large group of sandalwood trees. He stayed there

You have taken refuge in Sri Ramakrishna. You are young and pure. What infinite possibilities are before you. Why do you not try hard to follow our advice and learn to love and do the things we ask you to do? Learn to make your heart and your lips one, and let not your mind deceive you. Swamiji's ideal was, "Liberation for one's self and service to mankind!" With one hand hold on to the feet of the Lord, and with the other do his work.

FIRST OF ALL, the mind, which is the ruler of the senses, must be controlled. After that the mind and the intellect must be merged in the Atman. When you are in the society of holy men, you may think that your passions are dead, but do not be deceived. You are free of passions only after you have attained samadhi. Therefore be always vigilant until you have transcended the mind.

God is. Religion is true. These truths are not preached merely to make men moral or to keep an orderly society. God truly is; he is the Reality and he can be realized. He is *true.* There is no greater truth than he. Be calm, tranquil, and self-controlled.

Meditate four times regularly each day. The best times are early in the morning, at midday, at sunset,

for a while, and then he began to think: "The monk told me to go deeper into the wood; he did not tell me to stop here." So he continued his journey, and as he went farther and farther into the wood he discovered first a silver mine, then a gold mine, until at last he came upon a mine filled with diamonds and other precious stones.

and at midnight. Be steadfast in your ideal even when the mind is restless. Keep up the regularity of your practices under all conditions. Study the Gita every day. By such study the mind can be cleansed of all unnecessary thoughts and anxieties. This I know from personal experience.

Devote some time every day to self-analysis. Ask yourself: "Why have I come here? How am I passing my time? Do I really want God? Am I really struggling to find him?" A man's mind tries to deceive him, but he must not allow himself to be swayed by his mind; he must curb and rule it. Hold fast to the truth. Be pure-hearted. The purer you become the more will your mind be absorbed in God. You will be able to see the subtle deceptions of the mind, and you will be able to root them out. Who are your enemies? Your own senses. But if you can control them they will become your friends. Your mind is your only enemy, and your mind is your only friend. The man who analyzes himself thus can wipe out the subtle deceptions of the mind, and by so doing move rapidly along the path of spirituality.

Plunge yourself into the practice of japam and meditation. The mind is gross and feeds on gross objects, but as you practice japam and meditation, the mind will become subtle and learn to grasp subtle truths.

Practice, practice, practice. Find out for yourself whether there is really a God. A little physical austerity also is good sometimes. For instance, on the day of the new moon, or on the eleventh day after the new or the full moon, eat only one meal. Never waste your time in unnecessary talk. Remember God constantly. Remember him when you eat, when you sit, when you lie down; remember him whatever you do. By such repeated practice you will find that, when you go to meditate, it will be easy to remember God and become absorbed in him. As your mind becomes absorbed in meditation, a fountain of joy will spring up within you.

Give no time to idle cares or idle talk. Idle talk wastes much energy. In the Upanishads it is written: "Give up all vain talk." Devote all your time to meditation upon the Atman. In the Gita Sri Krishna says:

> Give me your whole heart,
> Love and adore me,
> Worship me always,
> Bow to me only,
> And you shall find me.

And Sri Ramakrishna used to say: "Never squander the energies of your mind." This means, remember God constantly. The worldly man is very careful not to squander his money, but he gives little heed to how he squanders his mind. There is nothing greater nor easier than the constant remembrance of God. Such a practice awakens the kundalini; the veils of maya are removed one after another, and a new vision opens up. Then you will see the wonderful treasure that lies hidden within you. You will unfold your own divinity.

As a general rule, a man's mind runs downward like a river—toward lust and gold, name and fame. Change the current, and make the mind flow upward toward God. The mind of Sri Ramakrishna dwelt always on the transcendental plane. Only with much difficulty could he bring his mind down to normal consciousness and to the things of the world.

Japam—japam—japam! Even while you work, practice japam. Keep the name of the Lord spinning in the midst of all your activities. If you can do this, all the burning of the heart will be soothed. Many sinners have become pure and free and divine by taking refuge in the name of God. Have intense faith in God and in his name; know that they are not different. He dwells in the hearts of his devotees. Call on him earnestly. Pray to him: "Reveal your grace to me. Give me faith and devotion." Pray earnestly. Make your mind and your lips one.

Cover everything with God. And, as you learn to see him everywhere, you will become "humbler than a blade of grass." See him in all creatures. Hear only of God and talk only of him. Shun that place where his name is not uttered as you would a graveyard.

Repeat his name and call upon him. He is very near, and he is dear to all. Why should he not reveal himself? Open your heart to him. He will guide you along the right path. There is nothing more purifying than his name and meditation upon him. He is our very own. He easily becomes revealed to us.

There is the path of devotion and there is the path

of knowledge. A devotee likes the form of God. He calls upon him, he sings his praise, he chants his name and sees his shining form. Sometimes he weeps and sometimes he laughs. The followers of the path of knowledge seek for the Light, and they become illumined. However, one is not different from the other. In the end, the devotee and the man of knowledge become one. Ignorance is destroyed by following the path of knowledge. The light of knowledge alone shines. What lies beyond the light of knowledge? He alone knows who goes beyond, none else. And no one can reveal that.

Have patience, infinite patience, until you reach the Reality. In the primary stage, meditation is tiresome—it is like learning the alphabet. Gradually, peace comes. There are boys who after they have been initiated complain to me that they are not getting anywhere. I do not listen to them for two or three years. Then later they come and tell me: "Yes, Maharaj, I am getting somewhere now." Do not be impatient. Struggle intensely for two or three years, and your heart will be flooded with joy.

Maharaj, we are university students, and have come to you for spiritual advice.

Learn to speak the truth always, and observe continence.

We have been practicing breathing exercises. Should we continue these practices?

No! Breathing exercises in themselves can be extremely dangerous. It is sufficient if you will repeat the name of the Lord. Through the practice of japam and meditation you will reach the stage of *kumbhaka* without risking the dangers which may easily come from the practice of breathing exercises. Practice japam, and your breathing will become finer and finer, and you will gain control of the vital energy in a natural way.

IT IS NOT AN EASY TASK to wholly surrender oneself, body, mind, and soul, to God. "How can I surrender myself to God? I have not known him nor seen him, therefore how can I love him?" These are the doubts that arise in the mind.

Once a man admitted to Sri Ramakrishna that he felt no inclination to meditate on God. The Master asked him whom or what he loved most in the world, and the man told him that he had a pet lamb which he loved very dearly. "All right!" said the Master, "That is very good! everytime you feed your lamb, every time you pet him or do anything for him, think that you are serving the Lord. If you can do this with wholehearted sincerity, you will reach the highest!"

Blessed are those who have received the grace of an illumined guru. The guru shows the way to the other shore, and removes all the obstacles. Have intense faith in the words of the guru, and follow his precepts faithfully. Thus will the impurities of the mind be washed away and the light of knowledge dawn. Enlightenment comes quickly to one who has faith in the guru. But one must learn to see God in the guru. The guru must never be regarded as man. By worshiping him and serving him as God, the body and mind are purified. Through the help of the guru, God is first revealed, and then guru and God become one. Unless the heart and mind are pure the vision of God does not come.

Sri Ramakrishna used to say: "When a man finds an illumined guru, he is soon freed from the sense of ego, and he himself becomes illumined." But no man can free himself from the bonds of worldliness if he follows an ignorant teacher. There is suffering for both the disciple and the teacher. For how can he who is not illumined give illumination to another? How can he who has not found God and received his command, who has not been strengthened by the strength of God, give strength and help to another? How can the blind lead the blind? Only a free soul can give freedom to another.

If a man truly longs for God, if he sincerely desires to practice spiritual disciplines, he is bound to find an illumined guru. That disciple who has the grace of the guru knows the path. Let him follow it diligently.

My boys, you have the grace of the guru. You have the desire for spiritual knowledge. By receiving the

Lord's name you have received his grace, and you also have the society of the holy. Now you must strive to get the grace of your own mind. By gaining mastery over your own mind, you will, by its grace, realize the grace of God and the grace of the guru.

The tendency of the lower mind is downward, toward worldliness. This tendency must somehow be controlled. Hold the reins tightly. As the expert trainer controls and trains the elephant, so must you learn to train and control your mind. Be its master. Let it not control you. Teach it to give up all craving for fleshly enjoyments. When the mind is once freed from craving it becomes your slave. That is why the ideal of renunciation is so highly extolled in the Gita and other scriptures.

God and the lust for worldly enjoyments cannot go together. To have one you have to let go the other. At the same time it is not possible to entirely give up the lower pleasures unless you have tasted the joy of the higher. That is why I insist that you give your whole heart to God now, while you are young. Make him your own. "God is my all in all." Fix this truth firmly in your hearts, and the path will be easy. When once you taste the joy of the Lord, all other pleasures will become insipid. Dedicate your lives to him. Take refuge in him only, and then let him do with you what he wills.

WITHIN EACH ONE OF US there is free will. This freedom of the will is in reality the freedom of the Atman within. Sri Ramakrishna used to say: "Awaken the power of that Self which is within you." After all, what is the meaning and purpose of spiritual practices and disciplines? It is to strengthen this will, the will to attain God in this very life. As the mind becomes purer, the will becomes stronger. It is downright laziness to relax this will and think that in some future time you will realize God. Think of Buddha. What determination he had! After years of searching he finally sat himself down under a tree, determined to realize God then and there or die in the attempt. That is what is needed.

I will tell you a secret. You may not fully understand its meaning now, but in time its truth will dawn upon you. And this truth is that every man's will and mind lead him progressively toward good. Some are led along thorny paths and some are led along smooth paths, but all reach the same goal. Knowing this, there are some illumined teachers who advocate the following spiritual discipline: Let go the mind and will; let them wander at random. But always keep vigilant watch. Be the witness. Thus, if the aspirant really lets go and still keeps constant watch, even though for a time the mind may run after filth and vanity in time it is bound to turn progressively toward Good.

Ah! Who can fathom the infinite moods of the infinite God? Whenever we try to express him through our mind and speech, we limit him.

IT IS EASY to do great deeds, the deeds that bring name and fame. But it is by his small, everyday actions that a man's character is known. The true *karma yogi* does not work to gain publicity. No matter how insignificant his work may be, he throws himself wholeheartedly into the task, because, for him, his work has become worship of God.

Everyone wants to do the work he best likes to do, but that is not the secret of work. Whatever work you do, whether you like it or not, know that it is the Lord's work, and adjust yourself accordingly. Remember this, all work must be done as worship of God. Give three parts of your mind to God and apply the rest to your work. If you can do this, your work will indeed be worship, and your heart will be filled with joy.

Under no circumstances give up your spiritual practices. If you give up the practices of japam and meditation and engage yourself solely in work, egoism is bound to arise in you, and you will become the source of quarrels and disharmony.

(Someone broke a bottle.) Maharaj continued: Ah! how careless you are! Where is your mind? With such a restless mind nothing can be accomplished. Learn to perform all duties, great or small, with a concentrated mind. He who can concentrate his mind in action can also concentrate when practicing meditation.

This is the true secret of work: First learn to like

your work, but do not look to the results. If you can perform every action as worship of the Lord, then only will you like to work and feel no attachment to the fruits of your actions.

In the Gita, Sri Krishna says that it is possible to attain liberation through work only, but in order to achieve this one must have intense renunciation. All mental, physical, and spiritual energies must be concentrated. Then only can you reach God.

Be active, but keep the constant recollection of God. Faith! Without faith none can attain God. He who has true faith has certainly reached God. If you have faith in one penny it has value, but if you have no faith even in a gold piece, it has no value for you. He who has faith in God is freed from doubts. Without renunciation there can be no faith nor devotion. Renunciation is of the first importance; it destroys all ego.

PRAY TO SRI RAMAKRISHNA. He still lives. Pray to him: "You are mine and I am yours." Merge yourself in his consciousness; he will show you the path.

But Maharaj, do you mean to say that Sri Ramakrishna is still living?

Of course he is living! Are you mad? If he were not living, why should we lead such a life, giving up our homes and all our possessions? He *is*. Ask to see and know him. Pour out your whole heart in prayer to him; he will remove all your doubts and show you his true nature.

Do you see him, Maharaj?

Yes! Through his grace I see him. Anyone can see him if he has his grace. But how many are there who love him? How many yearn to see him?

It is not an easy matter to see God. Without a harmonious development of the mental, physical, and spiritual powers, religion is not possible. Faith, intense faith, is what is needed. He who has faith has everything. He who has no faith in God doubts everything. He who has faith in God overcomes all doubts.

Without dispassion toward the world, faith and love do not grow. You must have dispassion. To lose the ego in God is dispassion.

Maharaj, when I sit down to meditate I find that my mind wanders, and I think of many things. How am I to stop this restlessness?

Just as the Ganges has its ebb and flow, so is there an ebb and flow in spiritual moods at the beginning. But later, as you continue, there will come an even flow of the mind toward God.

Try diligently to check this mad outward rush of your mind. You can do this successfully if you do not try to meditate as soon as you sit down. First draw the mind back from its external pursuits by means of discrimination and lock it up inside, at the sacred feet of your Chosen Ideal. Then make japam and meditate. If you try diligently to follow this course for some time, the mind will naturally cease to wander.

The way of japam is the easiest path to follow. By constantly performing japam the mind can easily be made calm and steady, and finally it will lose itself in God. Therefore I ask you to perform japam regularly and often and at the same time meditate on the Chosen Ideal. This combined practice brings quick success.

Always practice your disciplines with unswerving steadfastness and let not a single day pass without them. Whether you like it or not, sit down at the appointed hour every day. If you can continue your practices for three years with unerring regularity, I assure you that love for God will grow in you and you will feel yourself nearer to him. Then you will be prompted from within to call upon him and him only. Then you will not be able to turn your mind in any other direction. It is at this stage that the aspirant feels the joy of spiritual life within his heart.

Without intense love for God, it is very difficult to practice spiritual disciplines in the right way, even after retiring into solitude. When you are alone, there is always a possibility of serious consequences. Therefore two of a similar type and temperament should live together, so that mutual help and guidance may be given should any spiritual crisis befall one or the other at any time. But, on the other hand, if there are more than two, confusion may arise. They may indulge in worldly talk. Such idle talk not only causes the mind to lose its higher tendencies and nobler aspirations but makes it forget God.

While undergoing intense disciplines it is good to cut down the quantity of food to a minimum. Japam and meditation are not possible on a full stomach, because the greater part of your energy will be squandered in digesting the food, and the mind will remain disturbed. That is why moderation in habits, in food, in recreation, in everything, has been so strongly enjoined by the Gita. "*Yoga* is not for the man who overeats," the Lord says, "or for him who fasts excessively. It is not for him who sleeps too much, or for the keeper of exaggerated vigils."

In this sacred monastery, how great are the facilities for spiritual practices! You do not have to concern yourself about food, or clothes, or anything else. All is ready at hand. Live here and apply yourself wholeheartedly to a life of constant prayer and meditation. No good comes of living like a vagabond, my child.

If you think that you can become a *mahatma* or a great seer by wandering here and there, let me tell you, you are mistaken. You cannot become a saint that way. Without unceasing practice you cannot have any religious experience; it cannot be had by trickery. If you sincerely long for God, you must plunge into meditation and become completely lost in God.

Maharaj, how may one control the mind?

Through gradual practice the mind has to be concentrated upon God. Keep a sharp eye on the mind and see that no undesirable thoughts or distractions enter in. Whenever they try to crowd in, turn the mind toward God and pray earnestly. Through such practice the mind is brought under control and becomes purified.

When you can feel and know that you are helpless and alone, that you have no other refuge but God; when you feel that you have nothing in life to look forward to, then only will devotion to God arise in you.

Practice japam unceasingly. Practice it with every breath. Practice it until it becomes your second nature; then you will find yourself chanting the name of God as you fall asleep and again as you awaken.

Know for certain that God can be reached—that his spiritual form can be seen and that it is possible to talk to him.

Practice these spiritual disciplines, and as you practice new visions will open up—wonderful, beautiful visions. You may see many aspects of God and many spiritual forms. Or you may see an ocean of light or a steady flame. There is no end to this

God-unfoldment, this knowledge of infinite Existence, infinite Bliss. Light, light, more light! Therefore, engage yourself in these practices. With great earnestness chant his name and dive deep.

Learn to acquire love and sympathy toward all. Overlook the faults of others. If you cannot help an evil man to become good, of what use is your spiritual life?

Learn patience. Anger is controlled through patience. Be patient, forbearing, and humble. Humility is a great aid in the building of character. Sri Ramakrishna used to say: "He who can forbear, lives. He who cannot, is lost." Again he would say: "Water accumulates on low ground; when the ground is high it runs off." In a humble man sweetness of character and other good qualities develop naturally.

Try to remember God constantly—even while you are working. In the beginning it is a little difficult, but through practice it becomes easy. Never give up struggling. Too many rules and regulations for spiritual life are no good. The main thing is sincerity and earnestness. If these qualities are in your prayer, it will surely reach the Lord. God looks into the heart and not into the words of a man.

People talk of enjoying this world, but what do they know of enjoyment? First become a god and then enjoy. Before that, all so-called enjoyments are the enjoyments of a brute.

If your mind has become pure and you live with pure thoughts, no evil can touch you.

Maharaj, there is the song, "I want to taste sugar but not to become sugar." Should that be the attitude of a devotee?

"I want to taste sugar but not become sugar," is for the man who has not yet tasted sugar. When a devotee begins to taste the sweetness of God, he will desire to achieve oneness with him.

Are dreams about enlightened men or divine incarnations real?

Yes, they are real. Dreams about enlightened souls, gods and goddesses, and divine incarnations, are real experiences. They are actual visitations. Many spiritual truths are revealed to one in dreams. The effect and impression of such dreams remain. But one must not speak of them to anybody.

IF YOU WISH to do good to the world you must be perfectly selfless. Worldly people are such that often if you do them good they in turn will try to harm you. You have heard of the great soul Vidyasagar. He lived for the good of the world, and those who were benefited by him were the very ones who spoke ill of him and tried to harm him. If he learned that someone had spoken ill of him, he would say, "Have I done him any good that he does me this harm?" That is the nature of the world. But the truth of the matter is, those who are good will do good by their very nature, and those who are wicked will do harm by their very nature.

Once a holy man, seated on the bank of a river, was meditating. Suddenly he saw a scorpion floating on the water. He took pity on it and with the palm of his hand scooped it out of the water. But as he did so the scorpion stung him. The holy man suffered great pain. A few moments later the scorpion again fell into the water. The holy man again helped it out. Again the scorpion stung him. This happened a third time. Presently, a man who had been watching the whole thing asked: "Why do you help the scorpion when it stings you again and again?" The holy man replied: "It is the nature of the scorpion to sting, and it is my nature to help. The scorpion does not give up its nature, why should I give up mine?"

The mind moves upward or downward. Jealousy, selfishness, desire for enjoyment, laziness, etc., determine its downward motion; faith, devotion to God, love, sympathy, etc., determine its upward motion.

THE CHANTING of the name of the Lord purifies both the body and the mind. Have intense faith in the power of God's name and meditate on him. If you chant his name, all your bonds will be broken, and you will become fearless. You will find immortality.

The one object of spiritual disciplines is to know God—to obtain his grace. The mud of "lust and gold" that stains the mind must be washed away. Unless the heart is purified, God's grace is not revealed.

Sri Ramakrishna used to say: "So long as the needle is covered with mud, it is not attracted to the magnet. But when the mud has been washed away, the needle is naturally drawn toward the magnet." The mud of the mind is washed away if one thinks of the Lord and meditates on him and prays to him with a yearning heart. At once the magnet of God attracts the needle of man's mind to him, and the moment the mind becomes pure, divine grace begins to flow. Through this divine grace God is revealed.

Sri Ramakrishna used to use the illustration of the policeman's bull's-eye lantern. With its aid the policeman can see everyone, yet himself remain hidden. If anyone wants to see the policeman, he must ask him to turn the light upon himself. So it is with God's grace. God is the Light of Knowledge, and in order to obtain his grace and see him, you must pray earnestly to him to turn that light upon himself. Then only can you see him.

As long as a man desires the things of the world, it is not possible for him to have any earnest desire to know God. As long as a child is absorbed in his toys he forgets his mother, but as soon as he tires of them he cries for her, and is not happy till he sees her. Similarly, when a man tires of the playthings of the world his heart yearns for God, and he struggles with all his mind and will to find him.

The desire to live a pure and holy life does not come easily. But know this for a certainty. The grace of God is upon all those in whom this desire is awakened. In the world man receives repeated blows. He suffers much, and yet the desire to walk the path of God does not enter into his heart. He knows full well that every time he puts his hand in the fire it will burn, yet still he does it. Not only so; he uses every inducement to encourage others to do the same and regards that man as crazy who desists.

Whenever a young boy decides to live a pure life, dedicated to God, it is almost certain that his parents and friends will do everything in their power to obstruct his path. If he should stray, no one cares, but if he tries to find God, everything is done to discourage him. Such is maya.

Can man know God by himself? Can the intellect grasp him? Surrender yourself to him; love him, yearn for him, seek refuge in him, be mad for him!

The one purpose of life is to know God. Learn to be absorbed in him. Activity is not the goal. Work without attachment is only a means to absorption in God. Meditate and dive deep. As you dive deep, you will know that God alone is real and that everything else is unreal.

When, through spiritual practices, a little awakening comes, do not mistake that for the goal. Do not stop! Move onward! Light! More light! Go deeper and deeper. You must see Him face to face, and talk to him.

Enough of study and argument! Now gather the forces of your mind and direct them toward God and God only. Plunge into the ocean of Bliss.

Do not sacrifice eternal joy for the sake of ephemeral pleasure. Worldly pleasures will seem insipid to you when once you have tasted the divine bliss.

You see many attractive sense-objects before your eyes now, but where will they be when your eyes close in death? These objects of enjoyment lead a man from darkness to greater darkness. Which path will you take? The path that leads to darkness or the path that leads to light?

Ah, my children, you have glimpsed that path of light. Do not turn back to the path of darkness. Sense-attraction is strong indeed, and if you yield to it, it will create indelible impressions of evil in your mind, and before you are aware of it the mind will drag you down and down. The only way to remain safe from sense-objects is to give yourselves up wholeheartedly to God. Be strong in his strength, and this very strength will free you from the net of maya. He alone has known God's grace who has overcome this world.

THE SAME INSTRUCTIONS for spiritual disciplines do not apply to all. The guru studies the temperament and tendencies of the individual and instructs him accordingly.

Beyond a few general rules, no individual can be told in the presence of another what particular path he should follow. I have seen, in the case of Sri Ramakrishna, how he would take each disciple aside and privately instruct him according to his needs and temperament. If you should want to ask your guru any question regarding your spiritual practices, you should do so in private.

However, I will give you a few instructions which can be followed by all.

First, have faith in God, know that he *is*. Be firmly convinced that to realize him is the only purpose of life. By knowing him man reaches eternal life and infinite happiness, and all the problems of his life are solved.

Next, practice continence. Without perfect chastity no one can hold fast to high spiritual ideals. To nourish the body, mind, and brain, and to secure their fullest development, continence is essential. In a chaste man a special spiritual nerve is developed. With its aid, his memory, his capacity for spiritual understanding, and his faith in God increase. He is able to experience spiritual truths which lie beyond the reach of the senses. That is the reason why religious teachers stress the ideal of chastity.

Thirdly, control the appetite. Take only that food which is nourishing and easily digested. Avoid food that excites or produces lethargy. Eat very little after sunset. The brain must be kept cool in order to meditate. Eat only to keep the body healthy; health is essential in the practice of spiritual disciplines.

Do not make a show of your spiritual practices. When you meditate, meditate in secret.

The most suitable hours for prayer and contemplation are those at the junction of day and night, and at midnight. Daytime has many distractions. At night, nature takes on a quiet aspect, so that night-time is best for the practice of contemplation. At dead of night the mind becomes absorbed in God with very little effort.

Sri Ramakrishna never spent the night in sleep, nor would he allow his disciples to sleep long. When others had gone to bed, and all was quiet, he would awaken them, give them definite instructions and send them to the Panchavati or the temple to meditate. There they would spend the whole night in prayer as directed, and during the day they would rest. In this way Sri Ramakrishna took them through their various spiritual exercises. He would often say: "There are three classes of people who keep awake at night: *yogis*, *bhogis* (seekers of enjoyment) and *rogis* (people who are sick). You are all yogis. You should never sleep at night."

You are young. Strive hard to taste the divine bliss. When once you have enjoyed happiness in God, where else will you go?

THE MOMENT you become absorbed in the contemplation of God, you will experience unbounded joy. Days and nights will pass away in the blissful consciousness of God.

Do not speak of your spiritual moods and experiences to anyone, least of all to those of a worldly nature. It may hinder your growth. However, if you exchange your experiences with one of a like mind, whose temperament is in harmony with your own, you may be helped in your progress. Both of you are travelers along the same path. It may be that your companion has already walked your path, and is already aware of its pitfalls. Benefited by his experiences, you may be able to avoid those dangers and difficulties.

Do you know why you should seek the society of holy men? Their experiences are a great help to a spiritual aspirant. When you visit a strange place, if you have the help of a reliable guide you will quickly see all that is worth seeing there; also he will save you from the dangers and difficulties into which a stranger is likely to fall. Similarly, from the company of advanced souls you will gather many valuable hints, and your efforts will be simplified.

This life may end at any moment. No one knows when. Equip yourself for the journey with spiritual treasures. To arrive empty-handed at an unknown place involves much suffering and sorrow. Birth is inevitably followed by death. At death you go to an unknown place, so you must prepare yourself for the journey. Always be ready for the great call.

Here you have every opportunity to grow spiritually. Struggle now to reach the Reality. Hold on to the Pillar. Have tremendous faith in yourself. Say to yourself, "I can know God"—with this faith forge ahead and you will reach him. Then your life will be blessed. Free yourself from the wheel of birth and death. Be his eternal companion.

Banish all fear and weakness. Never weaken your mind by thinking of past mistakes. Sin? Sin exists only in man's eye. In God's eye there is no sin. One glance of his and the sins of many, many births are wiped away.

You have come to Sri Ramakrishna. Hold on to him. You will have nothing to fear. Make a regular routine for your spiritual practices. You must have certain fixed hours for meditation and study. Under all circumstances follow this routine devotedly. Steadfastness is very important; without it no success is possible.

By steadfastness alone the mind becomes absorbed in God. Unless absorption is achieved, freedom from the temptations of the world is not possible. Lust, anger, delusion—these are strong foes. Be strong in the strength of God and escape from this net of maya.

Follow your routine. The mind may rebel at first, but do not yield! Then gradually you will find yourselves masters of your own minds. When you have gained control over yourselves, and your minds have become naturally absorbed in God, then you need follow no rule or routine.

Life, like a stream, is ebbing fast away. The day that is once gone can never be recalled. Make the best use of your time. If you leave it till the last moment, it will be too late then to cry, "Alas, alas!"

KEEP UP A CONSTANT COMMUNION with God; then all the depravities of the mind will vanish. Set apart a room or some place for daily worship; retire there every morning and evening. Perform japam and meditation and prayer regularly for as long as you can. The more you devote yourself to the contemplation of God, the more fruitful your life will become; the more attached you are to the vanities of the world, the more restless will your mind become. I pray to the Almighty that by his endless grace he may lead you in the right path!

Know this: without worshiping God you can never have peace of mind. Therefore, spend some time every day in the worship of God, in japam and meditation, and in singing God's glory. True devotion, faith, and knowledge, are the results of long persistence in spiritual practices. Many people turn to agnosticism when, after a lukewarm attempt at spiritual practices, they cannot realize God or attain divine bliss. The reason is not far to seek. These people do not feel sincere attachment to God, therefore they find it difficult to persevere in their spiritual practices. The disciplines prove too arduous an undertaking for them.

Without divine attachment and divine love the mind becomes dry and restless. The more you suffer for God's sake, the more peaceful will you become at last. "Persist cheerfully in your efforts," said Sri Ramakrishna, "then you will succeed against all odds." So plunge headlong into spiritual disciplines and persevere in them; do not shirk them, even at the risk of your life.

It is hard indeed to kindle any thought of God within the human heart without the fire of renunciation. I am certain that the more a man possesses this fire within himself, the greater is the peace he enjoys.

We saw a true and living representation of discrimination and renunciation in Sri Ramakrishna. As time passed we learned to know him more and more. We read of discrimination and renunciation in the scriptures, but we saw them personified in him.

You must not divulge the secret of your spiritual practices to everyone.

There is nothing real outside, everything real is within.

God should be imagined as vast and infinite. To gain an idea of the vastness within one should look at the Himalayas, or the ocean, or the sky.

True character cannot be formed unless a man becomes God-fearing, that is, unless he believes in God, in the life hereafter, and in other such principles.

It is as impossible to conquer lust or control the mind by the mere study of books as it is to walk on air.

So long as the kundalini moves in a downward direction, the mind of man is filled with lustful thoughts. But as it rises, the mind also rises and then moves toward things spiritual.

With the growth of tranquillity, a man becomes eager to behold the vision of God; he then delights in singing his glory and meditating upon him more and more.

Like the Buddha, one should be bold. See what a mighty renunciation he had! To realize God he gave up all his royal comforts without a thought. What a severe course of discipline he underwent! Then, when in spite of everything he could not realize God, he took his bath in the sacred Nirajana (a rivulet at Buddha Gaya), and sat down with this resolve: "Let this body go; but until I have attained illumination, I will not rise." And the illumination came!

GOD IS THE wish-granting tree. Whatever a man asks of him, he grants. But, such is the play of maya, man does not want to find the blissful ocean of God; instead he drowns himself in the quagmire of worldliness and thinks he is happy. Then as he meets with the sufferings of the world he feels that his life has been lived in vain. You are sitting under this wish-granting tree. Ask to become divine and you will become divine. Ask to become a brute and a brute you will become.

In the domain of maya there is both *vidya* (that which leads a man to God) and *avidya* (that which leads a man away from God). Vidya is spiritual discrimination and renunciation. By taking refuge in vidya, you take refuge in God; while avidya, which consists of lust, anger, greed, egotism, attachment, and envy, drags a man down to the level of a brute. If you cultivate discrimination and renunciation, avidya will be destroyed. If you yield to avidya, God remains far away and suffering will be your lot. There are both vidya and avidya. Man has the power to choose the one or the other, and on the nature of his choice will depend his success or failure in life, and he will reap the fruits of his choosing. Why blame God for your sufferings? Man falls in love with the pleasures of the moment, never stopping to discriminate, and the suffering which follows is of his own making. Put your hand into the fire, and it will get burned. Is that the fault of the fire? Sri Ramakrishna used to say: "The lamp gives light to all. By its light one may read the scriptures and another may forge a check. Is that the fault of the lamp?"

My master used to say: "There is a peculiar breeze called the malaya breeze. When this breeze blows, it touches all trees. By its touch some trees, having a certain substance in them, are transformed into sandal trees, while the others, lacking that substance, remain the same." So also there are two classes of men. As soon as those of the one class come into the presence of holy men and hear their teachings, they are awakened. They realize the evanescence of the world, and become eager to find God and to solve the mysteries of life and death. They at once devote themselves to the practice of spiritual disciplines. Such men are sure to reach enlightenment.

Then there is the other class. Even though you may hold high spiritual ideals before them, they do not respond. They think they will live forever and that the world cannot get along without them. They also imagine it is sheer foolishness to give up the pleasures of the world for the sake of the unknown. Thus they remain sunken in darkness.

There is the path of the good and the path of the

pleasant: one leads to everlasting peace and the other leads to suffering. Choose therefore the path of the good. Time waits for no man. Choose now! Waste not another moment! Try to mold your mind in such a way that it will not think of anything but God.

Pray earnestly to him with all your heart and soul: "O Lord, give me understanding. Free me from all sense of ego. Teach me to submit to your will. Make me your own."

Yearn for him. Since you have taken refuge in Sri Ramakrishna, be certain that you have his grace. Unfortunate indeed is he who, having this grace, fails to recognize it. Do not miss the supreme joy. Solve the mysteries of life and death, and become the eternal companion of the Lord.

Sri Ramakrishna is the avatar of this age, and he is helping every sincere and earnest aspirant. He is waiting for you. Make a little effort; spread the sails of devotion, and the spiritual breeze that is forever blowing will carry you to your goal. Do not look back. Go forward. Make your life blessed by the vision of the Lord.

EVERYONE IS SEEKING happiness. No one wants misery, yet the deluded man ignores God, the source of all happiness, and runs after the worthless toys of life. If you really want happiness, throw away these toys and yearn for God. He will run to you and take you in his arms. Seek the toys of life, and you will find them; seek God, and you will find him.

"Eat the mangoes, do not count the leaves." The sole purpose of life is to reach God. Reach him first. Pray to him unceasingly. Wake up; plunge into the ocean of nectar. Solve the mystery of life and death, and become immortal.

God has many names and many forms. He is also without form. It makes no difference by what name or in what form you worship him, but worship him. Lose yourself in contemplation of him. If you are sincere in your worship of him you will be blessed with his vision. Sri Ramakrishna used to say, "Sweet bread will taste sweet whatever way you eat it."

Have faith and dive deep into the fathomless ocean, and you are sure to find the eternal treasure, the pearl beyond price. Do not lose heart if, after a little struggle, you fail to find it. The ocean is full of precious pearls, but you may not find them at the first dive. Try patiently to dive deep into meditation; in due course you are certain to receive God's grace. If you wish to meet an important man, you must seek him through his ministers; similarly, to obtain the Lord's grace, you must seek the help of godly men and undergo many spiritual disciplines.

Know that he is dearer than the dearest, and then pray to him with a yearning heart for his grace and vision. Cry to him like a child; he cannot resist your tears.

Make the mind one-pointed like the mariner's compass. In whatever direction the ship may sail, the compass always points to the north and keeps the ship on its course. Keep your mind pointed toward God, and your boat will sail smoothly. A man who does this never loses his faith and devotion, even if he is thrown into an evil environment. The moment such a man hears of God he becomes intoxicated with joy. A piece of flint may lie under water for a thousand years, but it will still emit sparks if it is taken out and struck.

Like a fallen leaf tossed to and fro by the wind, the one-pointed man is content to remain wherever the Lord places him. He has no will or desire of his own. He can live in the world and at the same time dive into the ocean of knowledge and bliss.

A pure mind is like a dry match-stick. It ignites the moment you strike it, but, try as you will, you cannot light a match that is wet. Similarly, if the mind becomes soiled by worldliness, you will find it extremely difficult to restore it to its former purity.

Maharaj, in spite of all my efforts, my mind is still restless. How can I curb it?

PRACTICE JAPAM and meditation regularly. Do not miss even one day. The mind is like a spoiled child —always restless. Try repeatedly to steady it by fixing it on the Chosen Ideal, and at last you will become absorbed in him. If you continue your practice for two or three years, you will begin to feel an unspeakable joy and the mind will become steady. In the beginning the practice of japam and meditation seems dry. It is like taking bitter medicine. You must forcibly pour the thought of God into your mind, then as you persist, you will be flooded with joy. What a tremendous ordeal a student goes through in order to pass his examination. To realize God is a far easier task! Call on him sincerely with a tranquil heart.

That is very encouraging, Maharaj, but at times I feel that in spite of all my efforts I am making no progress. It all seems so unreal. Despair takes hold of me.

No, no. There is no cause for despair. The effect of meditation is inevitable. You are bound to get results if you practice japam with devotion, or even without it, for devotion will follow. Continue your practice regularly for a little longer. You will find peace. One's health also improves if one meditates.

Meditation, in the primary stage, is like waging a war with the mind. With effort the restless mind has to be brought under control and placed at the feet of the Lord. But in the beginning, take care that you do not overtax your brain. Go slowly, then gradually intensify your effort. Through regular practice, the mind will become steady and meditation will be easier. You will no longer feel any strain even while sitting for long hours in contemplation.

Just as after deep sleep a man feels refreshed in

body and mind, so will you feel refreshed after meditation, and there will follow an intense experience of
happiness.

The body and mind are closely related. When the
body is disturbed, the mind also becomes disturbed.
Therefore, particular care must be given to the diet in
order to keep the body healthy.

Under no circumstances should an aspirant fill
more than one-half of his stomach with food.

Meditation is not such an easy matter. When you
have eaten too much, the mind becomes restless.
Also unless you keep lust, anger, greed, and such
other passions under control, the mind will remain
unsteady. How can you meditate with an unsteady
mind?

You must practice severe austerities, but by this I
do not mean physical austerities, or the torture of the
body. Real austerity consists in the control of the
passions. Passion must never be allowed to raise its
head. But remember, religion is not for the eunuch,
nor for the one who maims his body.

Unless you meditate, you cannot control the mind,
and unless the mind is controlled, you cannot meditate. But if you think "First let me control the mind
and then I shall meditate," you will never succeed.
You must steady your mind and meditate at the same
time.

As you sit down to meditate, think of the cravings
of the mind as mere dreams. See them as unreal. They
can never attach themselves to the mind. Feel that

you are pure. In this way purity will gradually fill your mind.

As you continue in your meditation you may experience a divine light or you may hear the ringing of a bell or the sound of Om. Many such spiritual experiences may come, but pay no attention to them. They are of little value, except to indicate that you are on the right path.

If you wish to realize God, practice the spiritual disciplines with patience and perseverance. In due course you will be enlightened. When the time comes, the Lord will reveal his grace to you. Sri Ramakrishna used to say: "Until the time is ripe the mother bird does not break open the egg." Do not be impatient. Impatience avails nothing. Work and wait. This period of waiting is no doubt very wearisome. One moment you feel hope, then again despair; joy is followed by sorrow. So the struggle continues for some time until God, at long last, is revealed.

Maharaj, how does devotion to God grow?

Keep the company of the holy; listen to their teachings and mold your life after their pattern. But without continence and the practice of meditation you cannot grasp the spirit of the enlightened ones; nor can you understand the scriptures. Read the *Gospel of Sri Ramakrishna* and meditate on its teachings. The more you meditate on God the better will be your understanding of holy books. To hear about the knowledge of God is one thing, to live in God is another. But the knowledge acquired through realization is different from both.

If you have the craving for fleshly enjoyments or the slightest desire for name and fame you cannot reach God. As Nag Mahasaya used to say, "It is like trying to row an anchored boat." He also used to say, "It is easy to get name and fame. But holy is he who can renounce them."

Blessed is he who finds association with an enlightened soul. Vain is this life if one does not struggle to realize God.

Maharaj, there are some who believe that merely keeping company with the holy is enough. One need do no more.

No! Merely to keep the company of the holy is not enough. You must open your heart and ask them to solve your doubts. You must carefully observe their lives and imitate their example. It is a lazy man's attitude to think that all one need do is to associate with the holy. Needless to say, association is also very important. For in their company doubts are removed and pure thoughts are awakened. No scriptures or books can create such pure impressions or transform a man's life as much as contact with an enlightened soul.

Maharaj, Sri Ramakrishna has said that soli-
tude is an aid to spiritual growth.

Yes, that is true; but you should retire into solitude
only when you have attained some growth in the
spiritual life. To retire from human society before one
is ready is unwise. In this world of time, space, and
causation, it is impossible to find true solitude. True
solitude lies beyond the mind and intellect. It is iden-
tical with the Most Tranquil. Therefore, it is better
for a beginner to live in the company of holy men.

The other day you said that impatience was of
no avail; that we should be content to work and
wait. Does that mean that we must not yearn to
realize God immediately?

I must have said that in another connection. Yes,
you must yearn to realize him, but do not be carried
away by temporary emotions, nor give expression to
them.

To intensify your spiritual emotions you must hold
them within. If you give vent to them, they will ex-
haust themselves. Then dryness may follow.

The man of true devotion yearns for God without
becoming impatient. Even if he sees no light he will
not give up his devotions. Only those who love God
like shopkeepers looking for profit will give up if their
prayers are not answered immediately.

Maharaj, how can we develop yearning for God?

When your mind becomes purified by the influence of holy men and when you practice spiritual disciplines, yearning will grow.

Maharaj, how does one attain peace?

Peace dwells in the heart of one who loves God. Realize that your life without him is barren. Yearn for him, and peace will follow. When a man finds no peace in the world, dispassion grows within him and he is drawn to God. The more a man realizes that the world is barren, the more intense becomes his devotion to God and the greater is his peace. The greater the thirst, the sweeter the water. First create the thirst and then you will find peace in God.

How can love grow?

By prayer, meditation, and the practice of spiritual disciplines.

Can a man realize God while living in the world?

Is there anyone outside the world?

No, Maharaj, what I mean is this: can a man realize God if he lives the life of a householder?

Yes, he also can realize God but he has a greater struggle.

Should a man renounce the world if dispassion arises?

Yes, he should. Once true dispassion is awakened, it will spread like a forest fire. As Sri Ramakrishna used to say: When once a man of renunciation is released from the bondage of the world, he never wants to be caught again. He is like a fish that has escaped from the net.

Is it possible to realize God without a guru?

It is, but it is not so easy without a guru. The guru is one who shows the path to God through a mantram. He gives the secret of spiritual practices. He watches over his disciple and protects him. A guru must be a knower of Brahman.

How can one make the mind one-pointed?

By practice. Pray, worship, meditate regularly. Meditation for one or two hours a day is not sufficient. The longer you practice, the more your mind will become one-pointed toward God. Follow a routine with regularity.

The aspirant must begin his spiritual practice by offering mental worship to his Chosen Ideal—God with form. Then he must meditate on his shining form and gradually let this form melt into the Formless. God is with form, he is without form, and he is beyond both. Practice meditation in solitude and silence. Seek God and God alone. Renounce lust and greed, and make him your sole treasure. First renounce mentally. Outward renunciation will follow if you detach your mind from the transitory, unreal objects of the world and attach it to God.

Maharaj, what is the meaning of the Vedantic saying: "Brahman is real, the universe is unreal?"

It means that the universe of appearance is unreal. In samadhi the universe disappears. If you ask a seer about his experiences he will say: "All is infinite bliss there! There is no 'I' nor 'you'—there is only Existence—Knowledge—Bliss Absolute. The joy of that experience is unspeakable."

Maharaj, what is the proof of God's existence?

The seer says: "I have seen him. You also can see him." Sri Ramakrishna used to say: "Merely uttering the word 'hemp' does not bring intoxication. Procure hemp, mix it with the right ingredients, and then drink it, and after a while you will become intoxicated." Watch and wait. Practice spiritual disciplines, and you will be blessed with the vision of God.

Sometimes, as I continue practicing japam, my mind becomes blank. What causes that, Maharaj?

That is one of the obstacles in the way to spiritual growth. Meditation must be practiced along with the practice of japam. Meditation means a continuous flow of thought toward God. When meditation ripens, there comes absorption, and samadhi is experienced. The joy that is realized in samadhi remains forever.

How should I meditate? Please instruct me.

Hold the mind fast to the lotus feet of your Chosen Ideal.

In which center shall I meditate upon him—the center in the brain or the center in the heart?

Meditation can be practiced in both centers. I would advise you at first, however, to meditate in the heart.

But how, Maharaj?

Meditate upon him in the center of the lotus in your heart. (Maharaj then gave the disciple more detailed instruction concerning meditation. These details can only be learned personally from a guru.)

But, Maharaj, the heart is made of flesh and blood. How can one think of God there?

By heart, I do not mean the anatomical heart. Think of the spiritual center situated near the heart. In the beginning, as you think of God within the body, you will think of your flesh and blood. But soon you will forget the body and there will only remain the blissful form of the Chosen Ideal.

Shall I think of him exactly as he is portrayed in pictures or images?

Let the picture or image be merely an aid in bringing to your mind the living, conscious, and shining form of your Chosen Ideal.

Maharaj, what is really meant by "meditating on the meaning of the mantram?"

What is the meaning of the mantram? It is the name of God. You have a name. If I call you, your form also comes to my mind. Call on the Lord in this same way. Repeat the mantram and at the same time meditate on the image of the Chosen Ideal.

How does one perform japam? By repeating the mantram mentally or audibly?

When you are alone, you may repeat it audibly to yourself; otherwise repeat it mentally.

Maharaj, for the last few days during my meditation, the mantram has appeared in shining letters before my closed eyes. When this happens the form of the Chosen Ideal disappears.

You must not let the Chosen Ideal leave your mind —meditation and mantram must go together. However, your experience of the mantram shows that you are proceeding along the right path. That was an auspicious sign. The mantram is the sound-Brahman.

How should I begin to meditate on the Chosen Ideal?

First make your salutations at his feet, and then proceed. But, as I have already told you, you must perform japam at the same time. The mantram is charged with spiritual power. The truth of this will be directly revealed to you as you practice.

How can one get the mind absorbed in God, Maharaj?

Practice meditation regularly. The early morning is a good time for meditation. Before you begin your meditation, read devotional scriptures. This will help you to concentrate the mind on God. After meditation sit quietly for at least half an hour; for during meditation itself the desired effect may not be produced, it may come later. The mind often grows calm while you are relaxing after meditation and then spiritual experiences come. For this reason an aspirant should not occupy himself with worldly thoughts or engage himself in secular affairs immediately after meditation. It may do him great harm.

Practice, practice! Even though you may not like it, keep up the regularity of your practice. Even mechanical practice is a great help. Devote at least two hours every day to the performance of japam. Sometimes it is beneficial just to sit quietly in a solitary place amid beautiful scenery.

Maharaj, what should I do if, while meditating on the form of the Chosen Ideal, other forms of gods and goddesses appear before me?

Recognize this as an auspicious sign. Know that your Chosen Ideal is appearing to you in various aspects. He is one and he is many. Meditate on your

Chosen Ideal, but if he appears before you in another form, enjoy that divine vision. Gradually you will find that all aspects are dissolved into your Chosen Ideal.

There are particularly auspicious days favorable for spiritual practice—new moon, full moon, the eighth day after the new or full moon, and days on which special celebrations are held. On these days devote more time to japam and meditation.

Maharaj, the scriptures declare that one should worship the guru before one meditates. How shall I worship the guru?

First meditate on him within the heart, knowing that guru and God are one and the same. Then let the form of the guru be dissolved into the Chosen Ideal, and then proceed with japam and meditation.

Maharaj, you always insist that I must serve my father. Isn't it better to become a monk and serve you?

Indeed it is. But will the mere wearing of the gerua cloth make you a monk? You have a duty to perform in serving your sick father. I am asking you to serve your father, my child, and at the same time to continue your regular spiritual practices. Such service will help you in your spiritual growth.

WHILE SWAMI TURIYANANDA and I were living on Mt. Abu, we received a letter from Swami Vivekananda just before his departure for America. He wrote: "To devote your life to the good of all and to the happiness of all is religion. Whatever you do for your own sake is not religion." How wonderful is this truth! His words are engraved on my heart.

It has come to my notice that some of you think that the part you take in the activities of the Rama-krishna Mission is a hindrance to your meditation and spiritual progress, and that Swami Premananda and I do not approve of such activities. This belief has no foundation. You do not understand our spirit. No matter how busy you may be in carrying out your duties, you *must* practice regular japam and medita-tion. This point I shall emphasize again and again. Remember the Lord always—before you begin to work, while you are working, and after you have finished.

We have heard Swamiji often say, "Work and wor-ship." Can anyone in the primary stage live absorbed day and night in meditation? Therefore you must work, but work without attachment and for the good of mankind. If you do not work, evil thoughts and unnecessary cares will occupy your mind.

The Gita and other scriptures emphasize the ideal of worship and meditation in the midst of the activi-ties of life. I can confirm this from my own experi-ence. "Work and worship" is the surest way to spiritual progress.

You see this disastrous war which is now going on.[1] Out of mere patriotism, men give up their wives and

[1] Refers to World War I.

children and all their pleasures, and sacrifice their lives for a worldly cause. Yet you who have given up hearth and home, renounced all sense-pleasures, and surrendered yourselves at the feet of Sri Ramakrishna for the sake of a noble ideal—the good of mankind and the realization of God—you want to avoid a little work! Swamiji used to say to us: "If you think you are wasting your life in doing good to others, let it be wasted. You have wasted many lives before in vain things. Why not waste one more life for the good of mankind?" But I am telling you that your life will not be wasted. You will realize God through work.

In performing japam and meditation, sufficient time and favorable conditions are important, certainly. But those who are inclined to practice spiritual exercises will do so under all circumstances. Those who complain of lack of time or suitable place can never make any progress in this life. Cultivate the habit of constantly remembering God, whether you are idle or engaged in work.

This constant flow of thought toward God is meditation. Neither time, nor place, nor circumstances need be taken into account in this practice. Plunge in! Oh, the joy of it! If you once taste that joy, everything else will lose its savor for you.

Why are you afraid of work? Work for the Lord, but do so with a steady mind. Whether it be a great undertaking or a simple one, it must be done with the utmost care and attention. Those who are steady in secular work are also steady in their spiritual exercises. To work in the proper manner you must have a profound regard for your work and at the same time an indifference to its fruits. All disinclination for work can be overcome if it is dedicated to God.

It is when this secret is forgotten that the mind becomes disturbed. With a disturbed mind, you will not succeed either in spiritual life or in secular work.

Certainly it is easier to do a noble deed for the sake of name and fame. But by such deeds a man's real value cannot be measured.

To know the real man, examine his daily actions; for it is his everyday actions which reveal his true character. A true *karma-yogi* will lose himself heart and soul in any undertaking, even though it is of a very menial kind. He is never motivated by the least desire for popular approval.

If you work and forget God, egotism and pride will overpower you. Therefore I tell you: never forget God, no matter whether you are working or sitting idle. To maintain this attitude you must keep up your spiritual practices, no matter what happens.

Maharaj, I have tried in various ways to control my senses but I have not succeeded. How can I do this?

If you merely say: "I will conquer lust, I will conquer anger and greed," you can never conquer them;

but if you can fix your mind on God, the passions will leave you of themselves. Sri Ramakrishna used to say, "The more you move eastward, the farther you are from the west." Call on God and pray to him. Then the objects of sense will no longer attract you.

Your way of practicing japam and meditation is very superficial. If you practice casually, devoting only one or two hours a day to meditation, you cannot find God. Lose yourself day and night in his contemplation, in singing his praises and glory; only then will you be blessed with his vision. Dive deep, my children, dive deep. Do not waste your time.

In the primary stage, the aspirant should slowly but steadily increase his hours of meditation. Otherwise, if, because of a momentary enthusiasm, he suddenly tries to increase his hours of meditation, he will find the reaction difficult to bear. He will become depressed, and then he will lose the power to meditate. It is a difficult task to lift a depressed mind and turn it back to spiritual practices.

God's grace is supreme; without it nothing is achieved. Pray to him unceasingly for his grace. Prayer is efficacious. He lovingly hears your prayers.

Hold on for a little while. Do not give your mind up to objects of desire. You must exercise great self-control in everything. Objects of desire! They will follow you like slaves. Then, through His grace, you will find you have no desire for them—nor will you feel any attachment to them.

You have embraced the monastic life, renouncing everything. It does not become you to try to exercise authority over others. That brings great bondage. Whatever you do, know that it is the Lord's work you are doing. Look upon everything and everybody as belonging to Sri Ramakrishna. "Being deluded by egotism, man thinks himself to be the doer."

To tell a lie is the greatest sin. A drunkard or a man who frequents houses of ill fame may be trusted, but never a liar! It is the blackest of sins.

Never find fault or criticize others. Such a habit is harmful to yourself. By thinking continually of the evil of others, the evil will impress itself upon your own mind and the good that is in you will be overshadowed.

Play with God, sing his glory, enjoy the fun! Why should you criticize others? Associate with everybody freely. Be happy with them. Do not indulge in gossip. Only a wicked-hearted man busies himself finding fault with others.

Keep yourself pure and go forward, following your own ideal.

Learn to see the good in others. If a man has some goodness, exaggerate his goodness in your mind. Give honor to all, praise all. Do this and sympathy for others will grow. He himself is honored who honors all beings.

Never run down a fellowman or slight him. Everyone sees the fault in others. Give him your love, make him your own, and help him to overcome his weaknesses. A man is composed of both good and evil. It is easy to see the evil in others but a holy man is he who can overlook their evil qualities and help them to become pure and holy.

Remember, my children, you are holy men. You must always be calm, gentle, modest, and kindly of speech. Goodness and purity must flow through every word you utter, every action you perform, through all your behavior and movements.

I bless you, my children, that whosoever associates with you will find peace of heart. The sleeping God will awaken within them.

What are the spiritual disciplines? Always be truthful. Be self-controlled. Watch your speech. Envy no one. Hate no one. Be jealous of no one. Practice chastity. If one remains continent for twelve years, he attains the highest.

It is wise to go occasionally to places of pilgrimage and live there for some time. The holy atmosphere and change of scenery are aids to the health of the body and mind. These places are also conducive to meditation.

The heart must be purified. This world is full of pitfalls. Effort must be your motto if you want to grow spiritually. Keep watch over every small desire which arises and control it. Strengthen the will and everything else will be simple.

*Maharaj, some days when I sit to meditate my
mind naturally becomes tranquil. Again on other
days it becomes so restless that I cannot calm it,
no matter how I try.*

That is the play of the gunas. The mind is subject
to all three gunas. When the sattwa becomes established through practice, the mind will always remain
tranquil. You see there is an ebb and a flow in the tide
of the Ganges. In the same way there are ups and
downs in everything. Meditation also has its ebb and
flow. This is only in the early stage, however. Do not
trouble about it. Stick to your practices. When you
have practiced regularly for some time there will be
no longer any ebb and flow in the mind. There will be
a smooth unobstructed current flowing toward God.

Whenever you feel a predominance of sattwa, and
your mind is tranquil, leave your work and engage
yourself in the practice of japam and meditation.

At each place of pilgrimage there is a special time
when the spiritual current flows. If at those times an
aspirant meditates, his mind easily becomes absorbed
and he finds increased joy in his meditation.

But Maharaj, how does one know that time?

It is not difficult. A man who practices meditation
can very easily recognize it. Benares! It seems to be

apart from the world. It is a place of mighty spiritual consciousness. If a man lives there and practices spiritual disciplines, he quickly gets results. The mantram, the seed-word, unfolds there with little effort on the part of the aspirant. Here, Vishwanath, the Lord of the Universe, gives liberation to everyone, whether he be saint or sinner, rich or poor, great or small.

Maharaj: Do you pray or meditate?

No, Maharaj.

It is good to devote a little time each day to God. The only way to control the mind and find peace is to chant the name of God and meditate on him.

Please tell me how to meditate.

Meditate upon God within the shrine of your heart, or visualize him present before you. Worship him mentally. Just as the ritualistic worshiper offers flowers, and waves incense and lights before the deity in the temple, so should you offer all the articles of worship mentally to the living presence enshrined within your heart. Do not waste any more time. Begin this very day. Practice japam and meditation once in the morning and once in the evening for at least two years. You will find great joy; spiritual emotions will arise; a new vision will open up. You are sure to find some result in two years. Some succeed even in a year. Stick to it! After a while you will find such joy that you will have no inclination to leave your meditation. Get yourself a new seat and use it only for your meditation. Sit straight, keep the right hand over the left, with the palms up. Hold your hands near the center of your body in the region of the heart.

Read sacred scriptures. When you sit down to meditate, do not begin the practice immediately. For a few minutes, banish all alien thoughts and make the mind blank. Then start your meditation. For the first few years, the struggle is hard; afterward it becomes easy.

If a day comes when you have a lot of work to do, you may meditate only once, or you may finish in ten or fifteen minutes. If the pressure of work is very great, fix your mind on God for a moment, then bow down to him and close your meditation. You can do this in exceptional cases, but not always.

Before meditation wash your hands and face. Observe the two following rules of moral conduct: speak the truth and look upon all women as incarnations of the Divine Mother. If you do these two things, you will find all other moral rules easy to follow.

Devote yourself to God. God *is.* Do not doubt his existence. I am telling you, my child, God *is.* Know for certain that he *is.*

Maharaj, there are some who meditate in the shrine of the heart and others who meditate on the thousand-petaled lotus in the brain, but I like to meditate externally. I try to see my Chosen Ideal just as I am seeing you. Which is the proper way?

Meditation differs according to the individual temperament of the aspirant. As a general rule, the best way is to meditate in the shrine of the heart. Consider the body as the temple and see the Lord installed therein. However, when once the mind becomes steady through meditation, then the aspirant can think of God anywhere; either at his side, or behind him, or in his heart, or anywhere else. When the mind becomes absorbed, a shining light is first experienced in the mystic vision. With this vision, there comes a kind of higher and nobler joy, and the mind is reluctant to give up this joy and move onward. But if the aspirant goes further, the vision of the light will be concentrated into the form of the Chosen Ideal and the mind become merged in his consciousness.

Sometimes again in his mystic experience, the aspirant may hear the long-drawn-out, sacred word Om, and his mind becomes absorbed in that. There is no end to mystic visions and experiences. The more you advance, the more you realize that the realm of spiritual experience is unbounded, infinite.

There are some who think that they have already attained God if they see a radiant light. Do not be deluded in this way. You must attain nirvikalpa samadhi, where all consciousness of duality is obliterated. Some say that that state is the end of spiritual experiences, but I believe it is the beginning.

It often happens that the mind, after making some progress, cannot advance further. Why is this so?

That is the weakness of the mind. The mind is limited by its capacity. All do not have the same mental power, but it can be developed. Sri Ramakrishna used to say that the power of the mind becomes strengthened by the practice of continence. A mind so strengthened is not overcome by lust and anger. Passions seem trivial to it.

In the path of spiritual progress many obstacles may arise. Evil, subtle influences may hinder your growth. Hence *mudras* and *bhuta shuddhi* and similar practices are prescribed in the ritualistic worship.

You call each one of us to you and inquire about our spiritual progress and our difficulties. You always give us new courage and enthusiasm, Maharaj.

But you see, I am not always in the same mood. Sometimes I feel like entreating and imploring you to go on with your spiritual practices. Again, at other

times, I see that the Lord is everything: the Lord is
the cause, the Lord is the doer, the Lord is the instrument, and the Lord is the deed. He is all and everything. I see the Lord playing in so many forms. Then
who am I to give instruction? Why should people
accept my words? But, you know, my child, that
when the inspiration comes from the Lord, they do
accept my words and follow them.

Is grace conditional?

Sri Ramakrishna used to say that the breeze of
grace is always blowing; but you have to unfurl your
sails. He would also say: "When it is hot one needs
a fan, but the moment a cool breeze comes, you stop
fanning."

*How does one know whether a man is having true
mystic experiences or hallucinations?*

The true spiritual vision brings a lasting bliss, and
the mind is aware of the truth of the vision.

*What is the real function of mudras and other
rituals in formal worship?*

Rituals are great aids in the beginning of spiritual
life. They help to remove many bad external influences which hinder an aspirant's progress. You will

notice sometimes that, as you go to meditate, your mind is tranquil. Within a few minutes, however, the mind is made restless by evil thoughts. I had to suffer at one time from such influences. Sri Ramakrishna watched me from a distance and knew my condition. He approached me and said, "I see that something is disturbing you." He wrote something on my tongue and uttered some words inaudibly. After that I was immediately free from the disturbing state. If, however, the aspirant has advanced, these influences cannot touch him.

Isn't it difficult to live a purely contemplative life?

Do not give up because it seems hard. Try again and again. Through practice it becomes easy.

Maharaj, what is austerity?

Austerities are of many kinds. Once I saw a man who had taken a vow not to sit or lie down for twelve years. When I met him only five or six months remained of this period. Continuous standing for so many years had made his legs swell as they do in elephantiasis. When he slept he held himself up by a rope.

Some practice the austerity of standing all night in deep water in the winter and at the same time performing japam. Again there is the austerity of sitting in the blazing summer sun in the center of four fires.

Maharaj, is that what austerity means?

Good gracious, no! Generally men practice such austerities with the hope that in their next lives they may be born rich and find greater worldly enjoyments.

Do they gain their wishes?

God only knows!

What then is real austerity?

Those are not real austerities. Anyone can practice them. The body is easily controlled, but it is another matter to control the mind. It is very difficult to renounce lust and greed, to give up the desire for name and fame.

Real austerity is based upon these three principles: First, take refuge in the truth. Truth is the pillar to which you must always hold while performing any action. Second, conquer lust. Third, renounce all cravings. Observe these three principles. That is real austerity, and the greatest of these is to conquer lust. It has been declared in our scriptures that he who practices continence for twelve years can easily at-

tain God. This is the most difficult task. I can tell you
from my own experience that it is not possible to
meditate properly unless you keep continent. The
craving of lust is very subtle, and extremely difficult
to control. That is why a spiritual aspirant must always be careful in associating with the opposite sex.
Through continence a special power is stored up in
the brain. If a man becomes established in continence, he will begin to see the expression of God
everywhere.

But remember, it is not possible to practice continence without devoting yourself to the practice of
japam.

NOWADAYS MANY FEEL that they should devote
their lives to the service of their country and mankind. I believe this idea has taken hold of the minds
of our people because of the influence of modern
education. It is impossible to do any good to others
unless one has already built up his own character.
Those who have taken refuge in God and have received his grace can never make a false step. By their
very living they do good to mankind. Their every
word and action, the very way they behave, become
a source of good to all. Sri Ramakrishna used to say,
"First hold on to the pillar!" That is, first realize God,
who is the goal of human life. Know him first. Have
intense faith in him, then go and serve others. When
a man realizes God and works as his instrument, he
finds peace in himself and gives peace to others.

My master used to say, "God is manifest in the hearts of his devotees, his children." Therefore we must be pure in heart; his home is in the heart of the pure. He stays far away from an impure heart. When our hearts become pure and transparent, when all impressions of the past have been wiped out, then only will he enshrine himself in our hearts, then only will he become manifest there.

The pure mind receives a clear reflection of God. If the mirror is covered with dirt it does not reflect, for the Lord's reflection does not fall upon an unclean mind. You are all young now. Your minds are free from stain. Keep the shrine ready for him within your heart. Take care that nothing else finds room there. Be pure and tranquil. Realize him in this very life.

Read only the sacred books. Those books which do not evoke love and faith in God are useless. They only make a man vain of his learning. My child, if you wish to make your life blessed, if you desire your own good, then dive deep into meditation. Do not float on the surface but repeat the name of the Lord and dive deep.

Sri Ramakrishna was born in this age to teach mankind that dispassion is the ideal of human life. Man runs after objects of enjoyment and degrades himself to the level of the brute. If you want to make this human life worth living, take refuge in God. Give up the false happiness, and seek eternal happiness.

Renounce. Give up this world. Give up everything for the Lord. Make him your own. "You are our

Father, you are our Mother, you are our Friend, you are our everything."

When we shall give up worldly enjoyments and pass our days thinking of God and contemplating him, then only shall we make our human lives blessed and inherit true happiness.

Three conditions are essential for the realization of God: human birth, longing for liberation, and discipleship to an enlightened soul. Through the grace of God, you have been blessed with all three. Make the best use of them and build your character in such a way that your life is not spent in vain. Do not seek temporary pleasures, find the eternal happiness. Remember this one thing, it may be that in another human birth you will have the longing for liberation but you may not find the society of such enlightened souls as you now enjoy. It is a rare privilege, the result of great merit accumulated through many births. Through rare good fortune you have come within the orbit of Sri Ramakrishna. See that you do not waste your life in vain activities.

Faith! Have intense faith in the words of the guru and you will achieve everything. Without faith in the words of the guru, spiritual life is fruitless. Give yourself up to him as a kitten gives itself up to its mother. Then he will look after you, help you, and guide you.

How far can your intellect go? Take refuge in the guru. He, with his greater enlightenment, and sense of responsibility, understands more than you and will protect you from all pitfalls. No harm can befall a disciple who is under the protecting wings of a guru.

Man makes many mistakes in life until he finds God. But if he takes refuge in his guru there is less possibility of mistakes. Sri Ramakrishna used to say that if the father takes hold of the child's hand, there is no fear of its falling. Even so, if you make mistakes, the guru, in whom you have taken refuge, will wipe away all your impurities.

Without renunciation there is no peace. Be dispassionate. To find goodness and attain peace, give up everything for God. If he has the will, man can be dispassionate and realize God. Therefore, renounce all cravings and hold on tightly to him.

Renunciation has nothing to do with the wearing of the religious habits. It is not for show. He alone is a real monk who has given himself up completely to God, keeping nothing for himself. "This body, this mind, this understanding—I offer everything to you. They are yours. Make them your instruments." Pray to him unceasingly: "Lord, I do not know what is good or what is bad; I am yours, do with me as you please." Pray! Pray unceasingly. Let him be your only refuge.

Another thing I want you to remember: through the grace of the Lord you have come to understand that the goal of human life is to realize God. If people praise or blame you, if they honor or insult you, if you find any place in the world or not, if your body stands or falls—never move an inch from your principles or from your ideals. Say to yourself, "I must realize God in this life at all costs." If you can mold your life in this way, then I shall know that you are a worthy child of Sri Ramakrishna. Then I shall know that you have made your life blessed by coming in contact with holy men.

One other point I wish to make clear in this connection. Who is the real guru? He must be an enlightened man. If a man does not know the path himself, how can he possibly show it to others? Mantrams, of course, are always potent, but when they are received from so-called gurus who trade in religion and are themselves blind, they cannot bring real peace or illumination. You have come to the children of Sri Ramakrishna; you are blessed indeed! He who is honest, faithful, and devoted will have to come within the orbit of Sri Ramakrishna, where alone in this age real peace is to be found. He who follows the ideal which Sri Ramakrishna embodies will become heir to eternal happiness. The disciples of Sri Ramakrishna know all the paths which lead to God. Proceed along the path into which you have been led and pray to your guru with a sincere heart. He will guide you, wherever he is. After leaving the body the true guru lives on in the invisible realm; sometimes he reveals himself to his disciples, but at all times he helps and guides them, until they, too, attain illumination.

Struggle! Struggle, my boy. Shake off all doubts. Plunge into your spiritual practices as taught by your guru. Never make a show of your spirituality but always practice in secret. Sri Ramakrishna used to say: "When you meditate, retire into a solitary corner, or a forest, and meditate within the secret chamber of your heart." Make a little effort for a time, and you will discover what fun it is to live a contemplative life. You will be transformed. You have the protection of an enlightened soul. There is nothing to fear. You are sure to succeed.

How many hours should one who is living a purely contemplative life devote to study, worship and meditation?

Devote as much time as possible. Those who lead a purely meditative life should spend at least sixteen hours every day in japam and meditation. With practice you will be able to prolong this period. The more the mind is absorbed within, the greater will be the joy of meditation; and when once you taste joy in your spiritual practices, the desire to continue in them will grow. Then you will no longer have to ask how long you should meditate. Your own mind will tell you.

Before you reach this stage, you must see that you spend two-thirds of your day in the practice of japam and meditation, and the rest of the time in the study of sacred books and in self-analysis. The more intensely you analyze yourself the more you will understand the condition of your own mind, and you will be able to eliminate the subtler cravings. When you are able to free yourself from these deep-seated, subtle desires, when the mind becomes tranquil, then only can you become deeply absorbed in real meditation. The practice of japam and meditation brings the aspirant to this stage. Spiritual disciplines are practiced to bring purity and tranquillity to the mind. If you practice japam and meditation and the mind still does not become tranquil, or you do not taste joy in God, then you may know you are not practicing properly.

Sometimes the mind does not like to practice meditation. What should I do then? Should I occupy myself in the study of sacred books, or should I force myself to meditate?

The mind rebels against effort. It always seeks ease and comfort, but if you wish to attain anything you must force it to struggle. That is the only way to make your mind steady. If you find it difficult to sit for long hours, lie down on your bed and practice japam. If you feel sleepy, walk and make japam. Only thus can you steady your mind and make meditation your second nature. Should you give up meditation because the mind does not like it? If you go on in that way you can never learn to meditate. Regular war must be waged against the mind. To force the mind to obey you is the ideal of spiritual discipline.

Should one observe the vow of silence during this period of intense contemplation?

Both forced silence and wild indulgence in talk are equally harmful. What is the use of checking your speech merely? Check the wanderings of the mind, that's the important thing. Avoid unnecessary talk and keep your mind on God who is Silence itself. That is the real meaning of the vow of silence. Forcible restraint of speech brings evil effects.

Maharaj, I cannot do anything by myself. Bless me, that I may have faith in you and in the Lord. Bless me, that I may understand your grace and have it always.

Never lose faith in yourself. The Lord will do everything for you. Have faith in him. Repeat his name. He will reveal the truth to you. Do not be restless. Have patience, and go on struggling. Struggle, and you will surely reach the Reality. Waste no more precious time in unnecessary thoughts or metaphysical speculations. Pray to the Lord that cravings may never arise in you. The Lord's grace shines upon all. Strive a little and your eyes will open to his grace.

Why did God create us? So that we may love him.

GLOSSARY

ashrama. 1. A center of religious study or meditation; a retreat, hermitage, or monastery. 2. Any one of the four stages into which man's life is divided according to Vedic teachings: celibate student life (brahmacharya); married householder life (garhasthya); the life of retirement and contemplation (vanaprastha); and monastic life (sannyas).

Atman. The Spirit or Self, the immanent aspect of the Godhead. See also *jiva.*

avatar. A divine incarnation. According to Hindu belief, God as Vishnu descends into the finiteness of name and form in various ages to re-establish the forgotten truths of religion and to show mankind by his living example how to ascend to himself.

Baranagore. Site of the first monastery of Sri Rama-krishna's disciples, from 1886 to 1891, *ca.* two miles north of Calcutta, where the young monks devoted themselves to intensive spiritual disciplines.

Bhagavad-Gita; or Gita. Lit., "Song of God," it is the Gospel of Hinduism. Dated between the 5th and the 2nd centuries B. C., the Gita, which comprises eighteen chapters, is a part of the Mahabharata. In the form of a dialogue between Sri Krishna, the divine incarnation, and his friend and disciple Arjuna, it teaches how to achieve union with the supreme Reality through the paths of knowledge, devotion, selfless work, and meditation.

Bhagavatam. The famous Hindu devotional scripture, attributed to Vyasa. The Bhagavatam illustrates religious truths with stories of ancient India's saints, seers, and kings. Dealing in part with the life of Sri Krishna, the divine incarnation, it is especially sacred to the *Vaishnavas* (*q. v.*).

bhuta shuddhi. Lit., "purification of the elementals." A spiritual discipline in which the aspirant mentally dissolves the universe into Brahman. The practice culminates in a meditation on the identity of Atman with Brahman.

brahmachari. 1. A spiritual aspirant who has taken the first monastic vows. 2. An individual devoted to continence and other religious practices in observance of the first of the four stages of life according to Vedic teachings. See also *ashrama.*

Brahman. The impersonal absolute existence or Godhead, the all-pervading transcendental Reality of Vedanta philosophy. See also *maya.*

brahmin. Referring to the brahmin caste. As described in the Gita, the idea of caste refers to a natural order—determined by a man's *karma* and predominating *guna* (*q. v.*). The brahmin caste includes priests, pandits, philosophers, religious leaders, and is the first of four main castes.

Chaitanya. A great saint and spiritual teacher, born in 1485, in Navadvip, Bengal, who later lived in Orissa. A brilliant scholar, he suddenly renounced the world and became an ardent devotee of Sri Krishna. According to Bengal Vaishnavas he was an incarnation of God. His ecstatic love of God embraced sinners and saints, regardless of caste and creed. Sri Chaitanya stressed bhakti yoga as a way to God-realization with special emphasis on japam as a spiritual practice.

Chosen Ideal. The aspect of the Godhead selected by a spiritual aspirant, or by his guru for him. Through meditation on his Chosen Ideal, the aspirant gradually attains concentration of mind, love of God, and ultimately illumination. See also *mantram.*

Cossipore (Kashipur). A northern suburb of Calcutta, where Sri Ramakrishna lived (from December, 1885, until his passing away in August, 1886) in a garden house at 90 Kashipur Road. It has been acquired by the Ramakrishna Mission.

Dakshineswar. A village on the Ganges, *ca.* five miles north of Calcutta, where, in the 1850's, the Rani Rasmani built a group of temples, including the famous Kali temple. Near one of the temples is the room which Sri Ramakrishna occupied for a considerable part of his life.

darshan. Lit., "seeing, experiencing"; paying respects to a holy place or person by a ceremonial visit; also the blessing or purification felt in the presence of holiness.

Divine Mother. The dynamic aspect of the Godhead, which is usually represented in the female form. The Mother appears under many different names as the divine consort of Brahma, Vishnu, or Shiva.

gerua. 1. The ocher color, symbol of renunciation. 2. The ocher cloth of ordained monks and nuns.

Gita. See *Bhagavad-Gita.*

guna. Any one of three types of energies: sattwa, rajas, and tamas. The three gunas make up the universe of mind and matter. When the gunas are in perfect balance, there is no creation, expression, or manifestation. When the balance is disturbed, creation occurs. In the physical world, sattwa embodies what is pure and fine (*e.g.*, sunlight); rajas embodies the active principle (an erupting volcano); and tamas embodies solidity and resistance (a block of granite). From the standpoint of evolution, sattwa is the essence of form to be realized; tamas is the obstacle to its realization; and rajas is the power by which the obstacle is removed. In the mind of man, sattwa expresses itself as calmness and purity; rajas as activity, passion, and restlessness; tamas as laziness, inertia, stupidity. Man's mood and character vary according to the predominating guna. The spiritual aspirant must overcome tamas by rajas, and rajas by sattwa. In order to realize the Atman, sattwa must also be transcended.

guru. A spiritual teacher. A qualified guru is, ideally, an illumined soul, or well advanced on the religious path.

Hanuman. Leader of Sri Rama's army and a hero of the epic Ramayana. Hanuman is revered in India as the ideal devotee because of his ecstatic love for Sri Rama.

Holy Mother. Sarada Devi, 1853-1920, wife of Sri Ramakrishna.

Jagannath. Lit., "Lord of the Universe." 1. A name of Vishnu. 2. The famous temple at Puri where this aspect of Vishnu is worshiped. The image in this temple has long been identified as Sri Krishna, with his brother Balarama and his sister Subhadra.

japam. When a disciple is initiated by his guru, the guru gives him a special mantram for his own use in prayer and meditation. A mantram is a holy name of God. The practice of repeating one's mantram is called japam.

The Hindu devotee recognizes that all the names of God have an equal power. Calling God by many names may seem to divide him, but God is present in every one.

Through each name, his power can reach his devotees.

"Truth is one, sages call It by various names." The one infinite Being, who is infinite Wisdom, infinite Love, can never be divided. He is one without a second. Yet he has many aspects and many modes of expression. Each of these aspects symbolizes the infinite God. Each aspect has its own sound-symbol, its name. These sound-symbols have been evolved out of the deepest spiritual perceptions of the seers and sages.

The Hindus believe that when such a sound-symbol, a mantram, is received from a *guru* (*q. v.*), it is charged with the living power of God. The latent divinity which is within each human soul becomes awakened by repetition of the mantram and meditation on the aspect of Godhead which it represents. The aspect of Godhead which is worshiped by an aspirant is called his "Chosen Ideal."

To quote Swami Vivekananda: "Every sect of every religion presents only one ideal of its own to mankind, but the eternal Vedantic religion opens to mankind an infinite number of doors for ingress into the inner shrine of Divinity, and places before humanity an almost inexhaustible array of ideals, there being in each of them a manifestation of the Eternal One. With the kindest solicitude, the Vedanta points out to aspiring men and women the numerous roads, hewn out of the solid rock of the realities of human life, by the glorious sons or human manifestations of God, in the past and in the present, and stands with outstretched arms to welcome all—to welcome even those that are yet to be—to that Home of Truth and that Ocean of Bliss, wherein the human soul, liberated from the net of maya, may transport itself with perfect freedom and with eternal joy."

This does not mean, however, that an aspirant can worship God in one aspect today and another aspect tomorrow. It is imperative that he should hold to his Chosen Ideal. The young plant must be hedged round and protected until it has grown into a tree. The plant of spirituality will die if it is exposed too early to change of ideas and ideals. Devotion to one Ideal is absolutely necessary for the beginner in his practice of religious discipline. While meditating on the Chosen Ideal, one must repeat the mantram.

Japam may appear monotonous and mechanical when not accompanied by meditation. Nevertheless, it has a good effect. If one persists, the monotony will break, and the presence of God will be felt. Through japam, an inner joy and sweetness will arise which will help the aspirant to devote himself more and more to the perception of the Presence of God.

In his teachings Maharaj lays great stress on the value of japam. These teachings were given to initiated disciples, who had received mantrams from their gurus. Those who have not yet received a mantram from a guru may repeat the sacred word Om, or any holy name of God which appeals to them.

jiva. The individual soul or human self. Philosophically speaking, jiva is the Atman identified with its coverings—body, mind, senses, etc. Ignorant of its divinity, it experiences birth and death, pleasure and pain.

jnani. 1. One who follows the path of knowledge and discrimination to reach the impersonal Reality; a nondualist. 2. A knower of Brahman.

Kali. A name of the Divine Mother. Kali is usually pictured as dancing on the breast of the inert Shiva, her husband, who symbolizes the transcendent aspect of Spirit, whereas she symbolizes the dynamic aspect, the Primal Energy. Wearing a girdle of severed arms and a necklace of skulls, Kali holds the bleeding head of a demon in her lower left hand, a sword in the upper left. She makes the sign of fearlessness with the upper right hand and offers boons with the lower right—destroying ignorance, preserving world order, and blessing and liberating those who yearn for God-realization. Kali is the deity of the well-known temple dedicated to her at Dakshineswar, and was worshiped there for many years by Sri Ramakrishna.

karma. A mental or physical act; the consequences of an individual's actions in this and previous lives; the chain of cause and effect operating in the moral world. Each individual's karma is made up of potentialities which guide his motives and conduct in the present as well as his future thoughts and actions. Thus every karma becomes a seed of another karma. The fruits of karma are reaped in the form of happiness or misery, according to the nature of each thought or act. Although each person imposes upon himself the limitation of his own character as determined by his past thoughts and actions, at the same time he can choose to follow the tendency he has formed or to struggle against it. The area of choice or free will in each individual reflects the freedom of the Atman, the indwelling Spirit. Devotion to God, enhancing good karmas and mitigating evil ones, begins to loosen the bonds of karma. When a man achieves illumination, his acts cease to produce karmas. In the Vedas, karma means also ritualistic worship and philanthropic deeds.

karma yogi. One who follows the path of karma yoga, one of the four main yogas, or paths to union with the Divine: the path of selfless work, in which the spiritual aspirant offers every action and its results to God as a sacrament. The spiritual aspirant may also practice the attitude of considering himself the witness of actions and not the doer, regarding himself as the Atman (separate from the gunas, which act and react).

kirtan. Devotional singing or chanting.

Krishna. One of the most widely worshiped divine incarnations of Hinduism. Among the most popular of his forms are those of Baby Krishna; of the young Krishna playing his flute (beloved friend of the cowherd boys and milkmaids of Brindaban); and of the divine teacher of the Bhagavad-Gita (friend and charioteer of Arjuna).

kumbhaka. 1. Retention of the breath, between exhalation and inhalation or inhalation and exhalation. 2. Suspension of the breath, an attainment resulting either from breathing exercises or from a natural spiritual development. A concentrated mind is the effect of kumbhaka when artificially induced by breathing exercises. Kumbhaka is the effect of a concentrated mind when it arises as a result of natural spiritual development.

kundalini. Lit., "coiled up," like a serpent; the spiritual energy lying dormant in human beings at the base of the spine. When this energy awakens in a spiritual aspirant and passes through the centers of consciousness in the central spinal canal, it manifests itself in mystic experiences and various degrees of illumination.

luchi. A rich Indian bread, made from white flour and fried in butter.

Mahamaya. The Mother of the Universe. On the one hand, her divine play veils man's vision of Brahman, making the one Reality appear as the manifold universe. On the other hand, through her grace ignorance vanishes, and man realizes his identity with Brahman.

mahatma. A man of God; a great soul.

mantram. 1. The particular name of God, corresponding to the *Chosen Ideal* (*q.v.*) of the disciple, with which the latter is initiated into spiritual life by his guru. The mantram, regarded as one with God, represents the essence of the guru's instruction to his disciple, who is enjoined to keep it sacred and secret, and to meditate on the aspect of

God which it symbolizes for the rest of his life. Repetition of the mantram (*japam, q. v.*), performed regularly and reverently, results in purification of the mind, and ultimately in God-realization. 2. Sacred word, verse, or Vedic hymn.

maya. A universal principle of Vedanta philosophy; the basis of mind and matter. Maya is Brahman's power; in this sense, maya is eternally inseparable from Brahman, related to him as the heat of fire is related to fire. United, Brahman and maya constitute the Personal God, who creates, preserves, and dissolves the universe. In another sense, as Ignorance, or Cosmic Illusion, maya is a superimposition upon Brahman. Maya veils man's vision of Brahman, as a result of which man perceives the manifold universe instead of the one Reality. Maya has two aspects: avidya (ignorance) and vidya (knowledge). Avidya-maya, leading man farther away from the realization of Brahman into greater worldliness and bondage, expresses itself in passions and cravings. Vidya-maya, leading man closer to realization of Brahman, expresses itself in spiritual virtues. Vidya and avidya are aspects of the relative (within time, space, and causation); man transcends vidya and avidya when he realizes Brahman, the Absolute.

mudra. A symbolic hand gesture. The mudras in the Hindu ritual worship, designed to connect external actions with spiritual ideas, serve as aids in concentrating the mind on God.

Narada. A great Hindu saint, mentioned in the Rig-Veda and in the Puranas.

Narmada. A sacred river of India.

nirvikalpa samadhi. A term of Vedanta philosophy referring to the supreme transcendental state of consciousness, in which the spiritual aspirant becomes completely absorbed in Brahman so that all sense of duality is obliterated.

Nityananda. An intimate disciple of Sri Chaitanya.

Om. The sacred syllable representing the impersonal Absolute as well as the personal aspect of God; the Logos. Om is the undifferentiated Word which has produced all manifestation. Repetition of Om with meditation on its meaning is prescribed as an effective spiritual practice.

paramahamsa. 1. A monk who belongs to the highest order of knowers of Brahman; (*cap.*) a term often applied to Sri Ramakrishna. 2. A monk who belongs to a particular sect of the Shankara Order.

prasad. Food or any other gift which has been ceremonially offered to God or to a saintly person; it is usually afterward given to devotees. A recipient of prasad considers himself blessed and purified.

purascharan. The vow to perform japam a certain number of times every day, methodically increasing and decreasing the amount. For instance, the aspirant may begin on the first day after the new moon by repeating the mantram one thousand times. Next day, he repeats it two thousand times, next day three thousand; thus increasing the amount every day until the day of the full moon, when he reaches fifteen thousand. Next day, the japam is reduced to fourteen thousand, and so on, coming down to one thousand at the next new moon. This practice may be continued over a period of one, two, or three years, as the aspirant chooses, or the guru directs. In connection with the purascharan, additional practice of japam is sometimes substituted for other religious duties, such as almsgiving, or the performance of sacrificial rites. In order to facilitate counting, the Hindu devotee, like the Buddhist and the Roman Catholic, often uses a rosary or string of beads.

rajas. See *guna.*

Rama. One of the most popular divine incarnations of Hinduism, king of Ayodhya, and hero of the Ramayana.

Rig-Veda. The most ancient of the four Vedas.

sadhu. A holy man, particularly a monk.

sahasrara. The seventh and highest of the yogic centers of consciousness, located in the human cerebrum. It is symbolically spoken of in Tantric terminology as the thousand-petaled lotus.

samadhi. 1. The superconscious state, in which man experiences his identity with the ultimate Reality. 2. Absorption, the eighth limb of raja yoga, in which the mind takes on the form of the object of meditation. It is defined by Patanjali as a state in which "the true nature of the object shines forth, not distorted by the mind of the perceiver."

sannyas. 1. The monastic life, dedicated to the practice of complete renunciation of self and the attainment of knowledge of the supreme Reality. It is the last of the four stages into which the life of an individual is divided according to Vedic teachings. 2. Initiation during which the monastic aspirant takes the final vows of renunciation.

sattwa. See *guna.*

savikalpa samadhi. The first stage of transcendental consciousness, in which the distinction between subject and object persists. In this state the spiritual aspirant may have a mystic vision of the Personal God, with or without form.

Shankara. One of the greatest philosopher-saints of India, the chief exponent of nondualistic Vedanta.

Shiva. God in his aspect as Dissolver, one of the Hindu Trinity. When worshiped as the Chosen Ideal, Shiva is the total Godhead, the supreme Reality. In relation to his power—the dynamic, creative mother aspect of the Godhead (called Shakti, Parvati, Kali, or Durga, etc.)—Shiva is the transcendent Absolute, or father aspect.

Sita. Consort of Sri Rama, and daughter of King Janaka. Sita is regarded by the Hindus as the embodiment of the ideal wife.

Sri. 1. The word, which means "revered" or "holy," is used as a prefix to honor a deity, or a holy personality, or a sacred book. 2. The Hindu equivalent of the English "Mr." 3. A name of Lakshmi, an aspect of the Divine Mother.

Sukadeva. Son of Vyasa and narrator of the Bhagavatam.

sushumna. The hollow canal which runs through the center of the spinal cord in the human body. When the kundalini becomes awakened in the spiritual aspirant, it passes through the centers of consciousness which are located in the sushumna.

tamas. Lit., "darkness"; see *guna.*

Upanishad. The sacred scripture which constitutes the philosophical portion of the Vedas. The Upanishads teach the knowledge of God and record the spiritual experiences of the sages of ancient India.

Vaishnava. A follower of the doctrine of Vaishnavism, a religious sect of Hinduism whose members follow the path of devotion to God as *Vishnu (q.v.)* or Krishna. Follower of Sri Chaitanya or Ramanuja.

Vishnu. Lit., "the all-pervading"; God as the Preserver, one of the Hindu Trinity. As the Chosen Ideal of the Vaishnavas, Vishnu represents not only the preserver aspect of the Personal God but the Personal God himself. Among the many forms of Vishnu, a familiar one is his four-armed aspect, in which he is seen holding a discus, a mace, a conchshell, and a lotus.

Vishwanath. Shiva as Lord of the Universe. The Vishwanath Temple is situated in Benares.

yoga. The act of yoking or joining. 1. Union of the individual soul with the Godhead. 2. The method by which such union is achieved. 3. (*cap.*) One of the six systems of orthodox Hindu philosophy. Yoga provides a means of attaining the highest consciousness and final release from worldly bondage by control of the thought-waves in the mind.

yogi. One who practices *yoga* (*q. v.*)